Covering just over one-th...                                           e
out of the regular preachi...
London, and its homiletic...
a full commentary but a valu...                                      ...ne
familiar Read Mark Learn fc...            ... small group study
under the care of leaders who .... the time to study the biblical text
for themselves. The rising tendency to leverage sermons into material
for small group study is wholly salutary, and this is a wonderful and
helpful example of its kind. I hope it circulates widely.

D. A. Carson
Research Professor of New Testament,
Trinity Evangelical Divinity School, Deerfield, Illinois

The need of the moment is for men and women whose lives are
deeply shaped by the word of God. God is meeting that need by
providing skilled and faithful Bible teachers to walk alongside us
and encourage us as we hear and study the Scriptures. William
Taylor of St Helen's Bishopsgate in London is one such sure guide
and fellow disciple. This series of studies prepared by him on Luke's
Gospel will assist individuals and groups to understand what this
part of the Bible is saying, why we need to hear it and the difference
it makes to the lives of God's people (and the world!) today. Behind
these brief notes and questions lies a patient, serious wrestling with
the text by one who knows that God's word is good and thrilling and
life-changing. Every Christian will benefit from reading, marking
and learning Luke's Gospel in conversation with William Taylor.

Mark D. Thompson
Principal, Moore Theological College, Sydney, Australia

This series of books is superb for personal study, and for helping those who teach the Bible to others. I've been getting a lot to give away to others now. The level is accessible, the reasoning clear, the application careful. Faithful and concise, never missing the big picture. Excellent.

Mark Dever
Senior Pastor, Capitol Hill Baptist Church, Washington DC

The best thing about these studies is not that they are clear and concise – which they are. It is not even that they are thoughtful and thorough – which again they are. It is that they pulsate with Luke's original purpose so evidently that each study is faithful to God's word and strongly application driven. I am delighted that St Helen's have added Luke's Gospel to this outstanding series of Bible Study notes. I have no doubt that God will use them widely around the world to build up His church. We look forward to using them in Singapore!

Denesh Divyanathan
Founding Pastor of The Crossing Church in Singapore
President of Project Timothy (Singapore)

What makes these notes so valuable is that they help us understand each passage clearly in light of the whole revelation of God in Scripture. While aimed primarily at Bible Study leaders, there is much to be learned here by preachers as well as those engaging in a personal study of Luke's Gospel.

Andrew Cheah
Dean of St Mary's Anglican Cathedral Contemporary
Kuala Lumpur, Malaysia

*Read Mark Learn* has taught hundreds of us over the years to know our Bibles and our God better.

Hugh Palmer
Rector, All Souls, Langham Place, London

*Read Mark Learn – Luke* is a unique contribution to Bible Study tools. It takes the Word of God as the foundation for all theology and the need for its careful study very seriously. You cannot complete a study without knowing that God has spoken and that the reader must respond.

While this volume claims not to be a formal commentary, it acts as a superb commentary on the text, while drawing out the main theological themes. The structure of the studies are a model of all aspects of careful Bible investigation, and so they teach both the leader and the member valuable ways to approach the text of Scripture. The aim of each study clearly springs from the Scriptural text, and the themes and application are drawn deeply from the passage.

These studies are not for the fainthearted. They require a high level of commitment from both the leader and member, a virtue that is so easily lost in modern Bible study groups.

This volume feeds the most knowledgeable Bible student, splendidly prepares the group leader, and challenges and edifies group members in the great truths revealed in Luke's gospel. I will be recommending it to our Theological College students!

Archie Poulos
Head, Ministry Department
Moore College, Sydney
Founding Director
Centre for Ministry Development,
Sydney

The *Read Mark Learn* commentaries are loaded with theological insights and actionable applications with grace driven wisdom. Dive in, devour and delight in the wisdom offered in this essential resource for developing a thoughtful and biblical Christianity. In particular, this Luke edition balances sharp theological insight with precise invitations for discipleship and growth.

Daniel Montgomery
Founder of the Sojourn Network and author of *Faithmapping, PROOF & Leadership Mosaic*.
Lead Pastor of Sojourn Community Church
Louisville, Kentucky

# Read Mark Learn

## Luke

Volume 1

William Taylor, St Helen's Church, Bishopsgate

St HELEN'S
MEDIA
CHRISTIAN
FOCUS

William Taylor is the minister of St. Helen's Bishopsgate, London.

© 2016 St Helen's Church, Bishopsgate

paperback ISBN 978-1-78191-911-8
Mobi ISBN 978-1-78191-915-6
epub ISBN 978-1-78191-914-9

10 9 8 7 6 5 4 3 2 1

Published in 2016
by
Christian Focus Publications Ltd,
Geanies House, Fearn, Tain, Ross-shire,
Scotland IV20 1TW, UK.

www.christianfocus.com

Cover design by Paul Lewis
Printed by Nørhaven, Denmark

# Contents

Introducing 'Read, Mark, Learn' ........................................................................ 9
Introducing the Study Notes ........................................................................ 13
Introducing Luke's Gospel ........................................................................ 17

PART ONE (A) LUKE 1:1–4:13 THE SAVIOUR'S CV ........................................... 25

SECTION NOTES: LUKE 1:1–4:13 ................................................................ 27
Study 1:   Luke 1:1-38: Announcing the Saviour .................................... 29
Study 2:   Luke 1:39-80: Defining the Saviour's Work ........................... 37
Study 3:   Luke 2:1-21: The Birth of the Saviour .................................... 45
Study 4:   Luke 2:22-52: The Saviour of the World ................................ 53
Study 5:   Luke 3:1-20: Preparing for the Saviour .................................. 61
Study 6:   Luke 3:21–4:13: The Authentic Saviour ................................. 71

PART ONE (B) LUKE 4:14–6:49 THE SAVIOUR'S MANIFESTO ........................... 79

SECTION NOTES: LUKE 4:14–6:49 .............................................................. 81
Study 7:   Luke 4:14-44: The Saviour's Manifesto ................................. 85
Study 8:   Luke 5:1-32: The Saviour's Mission ....................................... 95
Study 9:   Luke 5:33–6:11: The Saviour's Offence ................................ 105
Study 10:  Luke 6:12-36: The Saviour's People ...................................... 115
Study 11:  Luke 6:36-39: The Saviour's Pattern .................................... 125

PART ONE (C) LUKE 7 AND 8 THE SAVIOUR'S SALVATION .............................. 133

SECTION NOTES: LUKE 7–8 ...................................................................... 135
Study 12:  Luke 7:1-35: The Saviour's Great Salvation ......................... 143
Study 13:  Luke 7:36-50: The Essence of Salvation .............................. 153
Study 14:  Luke 8:1-21: Responding to the Saviour's Salvation ........... 161
Study 15:  Luke 8:22-56: How great a Salvation! .................................. 169

PART ONE (D) LUKE 9:1-50 THE SAVIOUR'S SUMMONS ................................. 177

SECTION NOTES: LUKE 9:1-50 .................................................................. 179
Study 16:  Luke 9:1-27: The Saviour's Identity and Mission ............... 183
Study 17:  Luke 9:23-50: The Saviour's Mission and Identity Confirmed ...... 191

Group Preparation Questions ...................................................................... 199
Bibliography ................................................................................................ 217

# Introducing
## 'Read Mark Learn'

Blessed Lord, who has caused all holy Scriptures to be written for our learning: Grant that we may in such wise hear them, read, mark, learn, and inwardly digest them, that by patience and comfort of thy holy Word, we may embrace and ever hold fast the blessed hope of everlasting life, which thou hast given us in our Saviour Jesus Christ. Amen.

*(Collect for the Second Sunday in Advent
in the Book of Common Prayer)*

## BEGINNINGS

*Read Mark Learn* is the title of a collection of small group Bible studies which has been developed, over a number of years, at St Helen's Church, Bishopsgate, in the City of London.

The original studies, undertaken for the first time in 1976, covered the whole of Mark's Gospel in one year. In subsequent years, studies in Paul's letter to the Romans were devised for those who had previously studied Mark; the aim was to provide a thorough training in Christian doctrine. Finally, a third-year study was established, consisting of a complete overview of the Bible. Thus, over three years, members of the church have the opportunity of gaining a firm grasp of how to read and understand the Bible. They are firmly grounded in Christian doctrine and practice from the Scriptures, and so they are equipped for a lifetime in the service of the Lord Jesus.

After some years it was felt that a change was needed, and so material for studies in John's Gospel was written. As with Mark and Romans, this material was written primarily for the leaders of small groups, to help them prepare, but it may, of course, be useful to any individual undertaking a study of these Gospels.[1]

In all the *Read Mark Learn* studies there is a commitment to consecutive Bible study, with Bible passages being considered within the context of the scriptural whole. This is based on the conviction that when God's Word is studied *in context*, God's voice is heard as His Holy Spirit speaks.

## PRESENT ARRANGEMENTS

The format that we have found to work well is to have a pair of leaders for each small group, with eight to ten members in the group. The leaders are responsible for all the teaching over a period of three terms, each term running for about nine weeks.

Every member is expected to prepare for a study by reading the text carefully – there is no substitute for close and careful study of the text – and considering the discussion questions that have been handed out in advance. The leaders will do this preparation both individually and as a group, meeting together a week or so in advance of the study and using the study notes in these books and the suggested discussion questions, so that they have considered the passage well in advance of teaching it. A key aspect of the leaders' preparation group is the time set aside for praying for each other and for the members of our groups.

## TRAINING FOR LEADERS

We have found these leaders' preparation groups to be a very helpful way of providing training for leaders, of supporting them in their ministry of leadership, and also, of course, of developing our understanding of the overall message of the book we are working

---

1.    To date the following volumes are available in this series: *Read Mark Learn John*; *Read Mark Learn Romans*.

on. In addition, there has been the long-term value of training people to lead house groups in the future.

The strength of *Read Mark Learn* depends, in human terms, upon the calibre of the leaders. Without the leaders' considerable degree of commitment – as indicated above – the whole enterprise would fail. And so a high priority is given to training and encouraging leaders on a continuing basis.

## Additional Material

Additional material to these notes may be found in sermons preached at St Helen's church in the 'resources' section at the following link: www.st-helens.org.uk/resources/media-library.

Particular thanks and recognition for this Volume in the *Read Mark Learn* series should be given both to Sarah Finch and Claire Tunks who have edited and re-edited the material tirelessly.

# Introducing the Study Notes

These notes were written and revised during the process of preaching through Luke's Gospel, teaching the gospel in small groups, feeding back and together correcting and revising our understanding. This process of sharpening our understanding and our application of the message of Luke's Gospel is a continuous one, and we anticipate considerable revision following publication of this first Volume!

The notes are not intended to be a formal commentary on the gospel; rather, the aim is to provide useful pointers to the main themes of each passage, and to show how these themes fit in with Luke's wider purpose in writing his Gospel.

## Study Passages

It will be noted that some of the studies are quite long. In studying these longer narrative passages we have found ourselves disciplined into concentrating on the one main point, rather than seeking to read a significance into the details of the narrative which may or may not have been intended.

Bible study leaders, however, may feel that some of the studies are too long for their groups. If this is the case there are two possibilities. One is simply to split the study – but beware the temptation to speculate on the narrative details, which may simply be matters of historical record without any deeper significance intended. The other is to select the core part of the passage and summarise the surrounding material. (Some of our leaders do this to good effect.)

## SECTION NOTES

Chapters 1–9 of Luke's Gospel contain four major sections, each with a distinct focus. Like all the Bible writers, Luke has carefully structured his material in order to drive home his main points. In the notes, each section is given a summary, and then there are comments on the main themes covered in that section.

## STUDY NOTES

Each study has the following headings:

*The Context*: How the passage being studied fits in with the wider context of the whole gospel.

*The Structure*: How the text of the passage may be broken down into smaller parts. The main point of each part is stated, and from the titles it should be apparent how each part relates to the overall main point of the passage.

*Old Testament Notes*: Luke's Gospel, written against the backdrop of the Old Testament, contains many ideas and concepts that Luke assumes we will understand. Here the most important ones are introduced.

*Text Notes*: A brief commentary on the passage. More difficult verses are touched on, but the main aim is to see how Luke develops the main ideas.

*Key Themes*: A succinct summary of the key ideas raised in the passage. These are grouped by theme, and are not necessarily in the order in which they occur in the passage.

*Application*: One of the greatest errors in application is to apply the passage to ourselves immediately, without first thinking about the application that was intended for its first readers. The aim here is to identify the message for the original audience before driving that application through to the reader now.

*The Aim*: The main point of the passage is taken as the aim of the study. The Bible study leader should enter the study itself with a clear aim, which ought to correspond to the main thrust of the passage.

*Suggested Initial Questions*: Suggested questions for leaders to use in the group study. They are only suggestions. They have been tried and tested in small groups, but Bible study leaders will need to adapt them to suit their own situations. In addition to these questions, which are to help the leaders, there are preparation questions to help all members study the passage before attending the group studies, and these may be found at the back of the book.

# Introducing Luke's Gospel

## The Author of Luke's Gospel

In the opening words of what we know as Luke's Gospel, the author indicates his method. He has 'followed all these things closely for some time past', and he has compiled 'a narrative of the things that have been accomplished', based upon what has been 'delivered' by 'those who from the beginning were eyewitnesses and ministers of the word'.

It seems, then, that the author has operated as an investigative historian, drawing on authoritative sources in order to give his reader certainty concerning the content and meaning of Jesus' ministry. Though the author tells us to whom his Gospel is directed, a man named Theophilus - the name means 'One who loves God' – he nowhere provides his own name. The earliest record of a Gospel with Luke's name on the text is a manuscript dating from A.D. 175-225. One of the earliest lists of New Testament books from A.D. 170-180 (the Muratorian Canon) records the Gospel as being by 'The Physician Luke', and Irenaeus, at the end of the second century, writes, 'Luke, the companion of Paul, set forth Paul's Gospel'.

Luke's Gospel is part of a two-volume work, known as Luke / Acts. In the book of Acts the author uses the first person plural (we) in a number of passages (16:11; 20:6-7; 27:18), indicating that he was present with the Apostle Paul on part of his second and third missionary journeys, and also on his journey to Rome, to be tried before Caesar. Paul makes reference to 'Luke, the beloved physician' in his letter to the Colossians (Col. 4:14).

It seems quite reasonable, therefore, to assume that Luke, the doctor and the friend, co-worker and travel companion of Paul, was also the author of Luke / Acts.

## The purpose of Luke's Gospel

Being the author of the two-volume work Luke / Acts, Luke is responsible for writing more of the New Testament than anyone else. He indicates in the opening verses of his Gospel what he aims to achieve. His purpose is to provide his reader with certainty (1:4). As the narrative proceeds across the two volumes, the certainty that Luke desires for his reader becomes clear. It will be evident in three areas of understanding. The first concerns the *content* of the gospel; Luke *defines* the gospel for his reader. The second concerns the *credibility* of the gospel; Luke *defends* the gospel. And the third concerns the *communication* of the gospel; Luke asserts that the gospel must be *declared*.

## The Gospel's Content

That Dr. Luke presents Jesus of Nazareth as Lord and Saviour of every kind of person is indisputable. The Gospel opens with declarations of Jesus' identity and mission (1:30-33; 1:47; 1:68-69; 2:11; 2:29-32), and closes with Jesus' own summary of His ongoing work (24:45-49). The book of Acts opens with Jesus commissioning His disciples to witness 'to the end of the earth' (1:8), and closes with Paul in Rome taking the news of salvation 'to the Gentiles' (28:28). Luke presents Jesus as the divine Saviour who has come to offer salvation to all people from every nation. However, the two volumes do more than simply present Jesus as Saviour. Luke takes great pains to spell out the precise nature of the salvation that Jesus came to bring. At its heart is the forgiveness of sin for the individual believer, as Jesus the Lord is received by faith (1:76; 5:24; 7:50; 8:48; 19:10; 24:47). This clarification of what it means to be saved by Jesus is repeated throughout Acts. It is evident especially in the key gospel-defining sermons of Peter and Paul (2:36; 10:36; 13:38-39). Repentance and the forgiveness of sin for the individual believer lies at the heart of Luke's definition of the gospel. The believer is saved by grace, through faith in Christ (Luke 7:50).

Luke also clarifies the nature of this salvation: it is not only for life now (6:20-49), it is also the ultimate and final salvation from all the effects of the Fall (see *The Structure of Chapters 7 and 8* in the Section Notes for these chapters). Jesus is summoning His disciples to an ultimate salvation which will rescue them from this fallen world, with its sin, disease, decay and death.

## THE GOSPEL'S CREDIBILITY

### HISTORICAL AUTHENTICITY

Luke / Acts is notable for its contemporary historical, geographical and sociological content. Luke is clear from the outset that he is recording 'eyewitness' material (1:2). In both volumes his frequent mention of contemporary political figures, specific names and places, cultural habits and even meteorological details, provide his work with an undeniable ring of historical authenticity. But Luke is concerned to defend more than the historical credibility of the gospel. His account also provides his reader with a theological and a socio-political defence of his work's credibility.

### THEOLOGICAL CERTAINTY

In the opening verse of the Gospel, Luke explains that his is an account of 'the things that *have been accomplished* among us'. What Luke is presenting is to be understood as the fulfilment of Old Testament promise. This explains why, from the outset, both Luke and Acts are packed with numerous Old Testament references and allusions. Luke's use of the Old Testament does two things: it provides theological credibility for the work of Jesus and also interpretative clarity. Jesus is accomplishing and fulfilling the long-cherished promises of God. His arrival is not unexpected. His saving work is the fulfilment of God's long-promised redemption plan. What is happening has been spoken of, by God Himself and through His prophets, over thousands of years. Grasping this, the reader will have real confidence. But Luke's use of the Old Testament does more than point to the fulfilment of prophecy. In chapter 24 the risen Jesus talked with His disciples and 'interpreted to them in all the Scriptures the things concerning himself' (24:37). He made it plain that it was 'necessary that the Christ should suffer these things and enter into his glory' (24:26). We find the same thing in 24:45: 'he opened their minds to understand the Scriptures'. Thus, the Old Testament Scriptures are the 'interpretative grid' by which the life and work of Jesus are to be understood. The New Testament cannot be understood without the Old Testament; the Old Testament is incomplete without the New Testament. In this way Luke demonstrates that the gospel of Jesus Christ is theologically credible.

## SOCIO-POLITICAL CREDIBILITY

Luke's aim to establish the credibility of his account extends further than this. Luke / Acts also provides a thoroughgoing defence of the gospel against the accusation of the Jewish Establishment (Acts 24:5) – or of anyone else – that Christianity is socially or politically dangerous. This defence is most evident in the closing chapters of Acts. However, throughout Luke's Gospel the Pharisees are presented in their true light – as unreasonable enemies of the God of Abraham. Luke's goal is that his reader should be confident. He wants Theophilus to have confidence in the content of the gospel and also to know that the gospel is historically, theologically and socio-politically credible.

## THE GOSPEL'S COMMUNICATION

At various points in both Luke's Gospel and Acts it is made plain that the 'fulfilment' that Jesus has 'accomplished' is to be proclaimed to all nations. Simeon, the old man who meets Jesus' parents in the temple (2:29-32), indicates this as he holds the baby Jesus aloft. The risen Jesus insists on it as He meets His eleven disciples (24:37 and Acts 1:8). Paul sees his own gospel proclamation as a fulfilment of God's promise that there would be 'a light for the Gentiles' (Acts 13:47). And the book of Acts ends with Paul declaring, 'Therefore let it be known to you that this salvation of God has been sent to the Gentiles; they will listen.' (Acts 28:28) This is the third strand of Luke's purpose in writing his account: he wants his reader to be quite certain that the gospel must be communicated and proclaimed, with confidence, to the ends of the world.

Luke is concerned that Theophilus should be thoroughly convinced, about the content of the gospel, the credibility of the gospel – historical, theological and socio-political – and the urgency of communicating it to the whole world.

## THE STRUCTURE OF LUKE'S GOSPEL

While the purpose of Luke / Acts is self-evident (Luke 1:1-4), the structure of Luke's Gospel is less easily identifiable. This is strange for two reasons. First, Luke tells us at the beginning that he has written 'an orderly account' (1:3). Second, Acts is commonly understood to be tightly structured; it therefore seems right to expect to find structure in Luke's Gospel. Those looking for structure have tended to see Luke 9:51 as the mid-point on which the gospel hinges: from 9:51 Jesus set His face to go up to Jerusalem. If this is the case, then the first part of the Gospel has to do with Jesus' identity and mission, and the second with His journey to Jerusalem, His death and resurrection. These *Read Mark Learn* study books are written in the belief that structure (where the author intends it) really matters. The Gospel writers are not simply biographers. They have a commission – either personally from Jesus or from Jesus' Apostles – to record not only the facts of Jesus' life, but also their meaning and the application of that meaning. Thus the Bible authors are themselves the church's theologians who, under the guidance of God's Holy Spirit, have organised their faithful record of Jesus' work and words in order to instruct His people in practical Christian discipleship. In order to handle this God-given material rightly, the reader needs to cut with the grain of the author's work. Insofar as this happens, the application of God's word carries all the weight of the Bible authors' (and thus the Holy Spirit's) theology. Application will be driven by big truths about who God is and what God is doing. Where the structure, theology and ideas of the Bible author are ignored, application lacks convincing power. It tends instead to lean on the theological 'grid' of the reader or preacher. It becomes either predictable or man-centred, and frequently plain wrong.

Is it possible to identify more structure and organisation of themes and ideas within the two 'halves' of Luke's Gospel?

## AN OVERVIEW

## PART ONE: LUKE 1:1–9:50

In Luke 4:14, the author records Jesus' return to Galilee, and signals the start of His public teaching ministry in Galilee. In Luke 7:1, Luke writes, 'After he had finished all his sayings in the hearing of the people….' This suggests that Luke 4:14 – 6:49 may be seen as a section containing the public teaching of Jesus. The material of this section is devoted to unpacking the meaning of His manifesto, delivered in the synagogue in Nazareth (4:18-19).

Luke 7:1 – 8:56 is very tightly structured (see Section Notes for Chapters 7 and 8). The central point of Luke 7 and 8 is the account of the sinful woman who is told, 'Your faith has saved you; go in peace.' (7:50) The section is all about the salvation that Jesus has accomplished.

Luke 9:1-50 is also tightly structured, with Jesus' identity being recognised by His disciples (9:20) and confirmed by His Father (9:35). The central feature of the section is Jesus' summons to discipleship (9:23-27). At the beginning of the book, Luke 1:1-4, Luke had laid out his method and purpose. This leaves a section, Luke 1:5 – 4:13, in which the aim appears to be to identify the credentials of Jesus of Nazareth, and to embed His life and work firmly within the context of Old Testament promise. Who Jesus is, and what He has accomplished, fulfils what God had promised throughout the Old Testament, from Genesis to Malachi.

## THE STRUCTURE OF PART ONE (A) AND (B)

| | |
|---|---|
| 1:1-4 | The aim |
| 1:5 – 4:13 | The Saviour's CV |
| 4:14 – 6:49 | The Saviour's Manifesto |
| 7:1 – 8:56 | The Saviour's Salvation |
| 9:1-50 | The Saviour's Summons |

PART TWO: LUKE 9:51–24:53

In chapter 9 verse 51 Luke records Jesus' deliberate decision to journey to Jerusalem: 'When the days drew near for him to be taken up, he set his face to go to Jerusalem.' By this stage Jesus had already indicated to His disciples that He was going to His death (9:22), and He had discussed with Moses and Elijah (representing the Law and the Prophets) 'the departure [Exodus – see Old Testament Notes in Study 17] which he was about to accomplish at Jerusalem.' (9:31-32) These chapters, Luke 9:51–24:53, record Jesus' teaching on His journey, His death and His resurrection, and the risen Jesus' explanation from the Law and the Prophets of what He had accomplished. It *may* be that Luke has provided over fourteen chapters of material in one block. However, given the earlier comments on the structure of Luke, and the suggested organisation of 1:1–9:50, this seems unlikely. A more detailed analysis of Luke 9:51–24:53 will be provided in the second volume. At this stage, however, it is suggested that Luke has arranged his material thematically (and theologically) around the 'journey markers' of 10:38, 13:22, 17:11 and 19:28. These markers create five discrete sections, each with its own particular pastoral purpose emerging from the work and words of Jesus as Luke records them.

# PART ONE (A)

LUKE 1:1 – 4:13

## *THE SAVIOUR'S CV*

# Section Notes
## Part One (A): 1:1–4:13
## The Saviour's CV

In the opening lines of his Gospel Luke spells out his purpose in writing it. His goal is to give his reader certainty, by showing him 'the things that have been accomplished'. This helps to explain the way in which the main narrative of Luke's Gospel begins. The material that Luke records in 1:5–4:13 is heavily loaded with contemporary historical detail and also Old Testament references. Luke's aim is not only to describe what happened, but also to demonstrate to his reader that what happened was in direct fulfilment of centuries of Old Testament promises. These chapters set out Jesus' credentials, showing that His birth and early life are firmly within the wider context of God's purpose and plan, as God had declared them from the outset of the Bible.

But these chapters do more than that. In this section Luke interprets for his reader the detail of the coming of Jesus, as He accomplishes what had been promised by God in the Old Testament. Luke does this by recording the words of the angels, of Mary, Zechariah, Simeon, John the Baptist and God Himself, which provide the meaning of what is taking place. Thus, from the outset, Luke is providing certainty concerning the content of the Gospel that is eventually to be proclaimed to all nations. The chapters contain so many Old Testament references and allusions that it would not be possible to look into all the ones contained in any one study. It is suggested, therefore, that the study leader should focus on just one or two each time.

# THE STRUCTURE OF PART ONE (A)

| | | |
|---|---|---|
| **1:1-4** | Introduction | |
| **1:5-38** | Announcing the Saviour: | Zechariah 'did not believe' (v. 20) |
| | | Mary 'believed' (v. 45) |
| **1:39-80** | Defining the Saviour's Work: | Mary: 'as he spoke to our fathers' (v. 55) |
| | | Zechariah: 'to give knowledge of salvation' (v. 77) |
| **2:1-21** | The Birth of the Saviour: | historical setting (vv. 1-7) |
| | | theological explanation (vv. 8-14) |
| | | eyewitness testimony (vv. 15-21) |
| **2:22-52** | The Saviour of the World: | the baby in the Temple: 'my eyes have seen your Salvation' (v. 30) |
| | | the child in the Temple: 'I must be in my Father's house' (v. 49) |
| **3:1-20** | Preparing for the Saviour: | 'proclaiming a baptism of repentance for the forgiveness of sins' (v. 3) |
| **3:21–4:13** | The Authentic Saviour: | proven by the Father and the Holy Spirit (3:21-22) |
| | | proven in His family tree (3:23-38) |
| | | proven under fire (4:1-13) |

# Announcing the Saviour
# Luke 1:1-38

## CONTEXT

The Gospel's author is Luke, the 'beloved physician' of Colossians 4:14. He writes to 'most excellent Theophilus'. Luke's Gospel is part of a two-volume work – he also wrote Acts. Dr. Luke states the aim of his two volumes in Luke 1:1-4. He is writing about 'the things that have been accomplished among us'. He wants Theophilus to 'have certainty concerning' what he has 'been taught'. The aim of Luke / Acts is that the reader should grow in certainty about what has been fulfilled in and through the work of Jesus. In the closing verses of the Gospel, Luke records Jesus' final words: '... that everything written about me in the Law of Moses and the Prophets and the Psalms must be fulfilled (accomplished) ... Thus it is written, that the Christ should suffer... and that repentance and forgiveness of sins should be proclaimed in his name to all nations ...' (24:44-47). Luke's purpose is that his reader should grow in certainty concerning the content, the credibility and the communication of the Gospel.

## STRUCTURE

| | |
|---|---|
| *1:1-4* | Luke's aim |
| *1:5-25* | The birth of John the Baptist is announced: Zechariah 'did not believe' |
| *1:26-38* | Jesus' birth is announced: Mary 'believed' |

## Old Testament Notes

*Elijah:* Elijah was the first great reforming prophet in the Old Testament (1 Kings 17–2 Kings 2). He preached repentance to wicked King Ahab. The Old Testament concludes with promises in the book of Malachi that God will send 'my messenger' who will 'prepare the way before me' (Mal. 3:1). Malachi describes this messenger as another 'Elijah', and tells us that his work will turn the hearts of fathers to their children and vice versa (Mal. 4:5-6).

*'the Son of the Most High' / the Son of God:* The phrase 'Son of God' is another title for God's anointed King. The idea is found in Psalm 2:7: 'The Lord said to me, "You are my Son; today I have begotten you."'

*'the throne of his father David':* King David was the great king of Israel. God promised David that his throne would be established forever (2 Sam. 7:16; 1 Chron. 28:4). This promise is known as the Davidic Covenant. From the time of great King David, one of the major themes of the Old Testament is the anticipation of, and search for, the eternal King who will reign and rule on David's throne (Isa. 9:6-7; Ezek. 37:24-25).

*'the house of Jacob':* Jacob, grandson of Abraham, was re-named Israel. From his twelve sons came the twelve tribes of Israel. The house of Jacob refers to all of God's people in the Old Testament – Israel.

## Text Notes

### 1:1-4 Luke's aim

*The sources:* The author of the Gospel is Luke. He is described by Paul in his letter to the Colossians as 'the beloved physician' (4:14). Luke travelled with Paul and was with him for a significant period in Jerusalem (Acts 21:17, 18; 27:1). Luke had privileged access to many of the authorised witnesses of Jesus' life and teaching. He refers to them using the technical term 'eyewitnesses' (v. 2). It is a word used by Jesus to speak of the Apostles in 24:48: 'You are witnesses of these things.' We find the word in Acts 1:8: '... and you will be my witnesses...'. In Acts 1:21-26, when a twelfth Apostle is chosen to replace Judas, Peter insists that he must be someone who had 'accompanied us during all the time that the Lord Jesus went in and out among us, beginning from the baptism of John until the day when he was taken up from us….'

The phrase 'ministers of the word' (v. 2) is another technical term, meaning someone who acts under orders. It is used in the first century to refer to appointed officials in the law courts, the military and the palace. In Luke 4:20 we find it used to describe the synagogue attendant in charge of the scrolls.

The verb 'to deliver' (v. 2) suggests handing on something that has been entrusted to one (cf. Luke 10:22). We can check the careful way that Luke has handled his sources by looking at parallel accounts in Mark and Matthew. Luke is dealing with eyewitness historical testimony, and he is highly responsible with his sources.

*Luke's method:* Luke had 'followed all things closely for some time past'. It seems that he acted as an investigative historian, interviewing and checking his account with the original authorised sources. This is typical of first century historical method. Professor Richard Bauckham writes: 'the ancient historians such as Theucydides, Polybius, Josephus and Tacitus were convinced that true history could be written only while events were still within living memory, and they valued as their sources oral reports and direct experience of the events by involved participants in them… eyewitness testimony was the essential means to reach back to the past.'[1] Luke is an historian.

*Luke's content:* Luke tells us that he is writing about 'the things that have been accomplished among us.' The word 'accomplished' implies fulfilment. It is used repeatedly in the Gospel to speak of Jesus' fulfilment of everything the Old Testament anticipates (e.g. 9:31; 24:44-49). Luke is not seeking to impose his own meaning or agenda onto the life of Jesus. Jesus will be properly understood only as we grasp what He has done as an accomplishment of Old Testament promise.

---

1.  Richard Bauckham, *Jesus and the Eyewitnesses*, (Grand Rapids, Michigan/ Cambridge UK: Eerdmans 2006), p. 8 and p. 93

Luke's aim is to show his reader that what Jesus accomplished was what the Old Testament points to. Luke is writing 'an orderly account'. The account is ordered chronologically, from the birth of Jesus to His resurrection. It is also ordered theologically, dealing with specific aspects of Jesus' teaching and ministry. Luke is a theologian.

*Luke's goal:* Luke writes to Theophilus, whose identity is never disclosed. The name means 'One who loves God'. Here we are told that he 'has been taught' (the word is the word from which we derive 'to catechise') what Luke is writing about. Theophilus may have been a Roman citizen who is either a believer, or someone Luke wants to persuade to believe the gospel and then defend it.

The Gospel finishes with the risen Jesus teaching His disciples about the things He has accomplished, and insisting that 'repentance and forgiveness of sins should be proclaimed in his name to all nations'. This suggests that Luke's aim is that Theophilus should grow in confidence concerning the gospel, in both its content and its consistency, so that he will engage in its defence and proclamation to the ends of the earth. Luke is an evangelist.

1:5-38 Gabriel appears to Zechariah and to Mary

*God's word to Zechariah*

*vv5-8:* Dr Luke's skill as an historian is shown by his precision in verses 5-6. He often inserts detailed historical data into his Gospel, indicating that his work is not myth or fairy tale. Mention of Elizabeth's inability to have children evokes memories both of Sarah, wife of Abraham (Gen. 17–18), and Hannah, the mother of Samuel (1 Sam. 1). In both cases God acted miraculously to enable conception. Sarah's son Isaac became one of the great patriarchs of Israel; and Hannah's son Samuel went on to prepare the way for great king David.

*vv9-12:* To be selected by lot to enter the Temple for the evening sacrifice was a once-in-a-lifetime experience. There were thousands of priests available for the task; only one was chosen. Those chosen were never eligible to do it again. Part of the priest's responsibility was to pray for the salvation of Israel. Zechariah is in no doubt that the angel is a messenger from God. His fear and trouble are matched by Mary's (v. 29). The angel addresses Zechariah and Mary in the same way.

*vv13-17*: The significance of what the angel says is realised only with reference to the Old Testament (see Old Testament Notes). John will be the beginning of God's answer to Israel's centuries-old longing. Malachi called God's people to turn back to God. He promised a visitation from God. He identified God's messenger as a preparatory Elijah-figure who would summon Israel to repentance. Their turning would bring reconciliation between God and His people, parents and children, rebels and the righteous (Mal. 4:5-6).

## ZECHARIAH'S RESPONSE

*vv18-25*: There are many parallels between the appearances of Gabriel to Zechariah and to Mary, but there is a real contrast between their responses to God's word. Zechariah 'did not believe'. This contrast anticipates a major theme of the Gospel.

## GOD'S WORD TO MARY

*vv26-33*: Gabriel's message to Mary gives her the divine title of her son, and asserts both His human lineage and the eternal nature of His rule. The tight connections to the Old Testament are crucial (see Old Testament Notes). Luke is recording 'the things that have been accomplished'. The titles 'Son of the Most High' (v. 32) and 'Son of God' (v. 35) both indicate that Jesus will be God's anointed Ruler over God's people (Ps. 2). The 'throne of David' is the royal kingdom promised to David and, in particular, to one of his descendants. This eternal kingdom is precisely what had been promised to David. This promise had never been realised because of the flawed nature first of David and then of each of his human descendants. Now at last, in fulfilment of God's promises, the Holy Spirit will bring about a 'holy' (v. 35) descendant.

## MARY'S RESPONSE

*vv34-38*: Mary's 'How will this be …?' is quite different from Zechariah's 'How shall I know this?' Unlike Zechariah she readily accepts Gabriel's explanation. 'For nothing will be impossible with God.' (v. 37) has strong connections with Genesis 18:14. What

God did for Abraham and Sarah He is about to do for Mary and Joseph. This model response by Mary to God's word of promise is something Luke emphasises repeatedly in his Gospel (6:49; 8:15; 10:39; 11:28).

## Key Themes

*Confidence in Luke's work:* Luke is a responsible historian who has compiled a carefully ordered theological account.

*Clarity about Luke's aim:* Luke wants his readers to have such certainty about the content and credibility of what has been accomplished by Jesus that they commit to taking this message to all nations.

*Fulfilment of prophecy:* God's promise to visit His people and establish His chosen king over His eternal kingdom has been realised in Jesus.

*The correct response:* God's promise will require a response of repentance and attentive obedience.

## Application

*To them then:* In Luke's day the proclamation of the gospel met with fierce resistance both from the religious Establishment and from the State. Luke had travelled with the Apostle Paul and had witnessed hostility and unbelief not only in the synagogues, but also amongst the Roman rulers, the contemporary philosophers, and the masses. The rejection of the gospel by so many was a major stumbling block to belief and to confident global mission. Luke wants his readers not only to be clear on the content of the Gospel, but also to see that his Gospel is credible as an historical record of Jesus, and that what he is reporting has roots reaching right back into the earliest parts of the Old Testament. The promises of God concerning His kingdom and His king have been realised in Jesus. Luke wants his readers, like Mary, to take God's word seriously.

*To us now:* The challenges to our faith and to our confidence in mission are just as real today as they were in the first century. Luke's explanation of his research methods and of his aim should give us certainty that we are dealing with historical facts, not fanciful make-believe. We should be clear on the kind of material we are dealing with. This is both an historical and a theological document. It has to do with all that has been accomplished in Jesus. Jesus is the long-promised king over God's eternal kingdom. Our study of the Gospel should give us confidence in the content, the credibility (historical, theological and socio-political) and the communication of the Gospel. We should look at the contrast between Zechariah's and Mary's responses and seek to copy Mary.

## THE AIM

The aim of this study is that we should see Luke's Gospel as an historical narrative of the fulfilment of God's promises concerning His king and His kingdom, and so have confidence in it.

## SUGGESTED INITIAL QUESTIONS

✤ 1:1-4

↘ What do we learn here about Dr Luke's sources, method, content and goal?

↘ How does what Luke tells us here challenge popular ideas about the reliability of the gospel accounts?

↘ Look up 24:4-48. How does Jesus' reference here to eyewitnesses, and to what He has accomplished, help us understand the aim of Luke's Gospel?

↘ Write your own short sentence (no more than twenty words) expressing what Luke is seeking to achieve.

✤ 1:5-25

↘ From these verses what do we learn about Zechariah, Elizabeth, the people of God, and John?

↘ Read Malachi 3:1 and 4:5-6. How does what the angel Gabriel says to Zechariah tie in with what God promises in Malachi?

↘ What does Zechariah do wrong?

✤ 1:26-38

↘ What do these verses tell us about Jesus?

↘ Look up 2 Samuel 7:16, Psalm 2:7 and Isaiah 9:6-7. How does what the angel Gabriel says to Mary tie in with what God promises in these passages?

↘ What does Mary do right?

## SUMMARY

How does what we see in God's announcements to Zechariah and to Mary establish confidence in the content and credibility of the gospel?

# Defining the Saviour's Work
## Luke 1:39-80

## THE CONTEXT

Luke's aim (1:1-4) is that his readers should be certain about the things they have been taught. These things have to do with the fulfilment of all God's promises in the person of Jesus (1:1). Luke wants his readers to become more and more certain, about both the content and the credibility of the gospel, so that the true gospel will be proclaimed to the nations. The births of John the Baptist and Jesus have already been presented in the context of great Old Testament themes. The Baptist is to act as an Elijah figure preparing the way for God's arrival. He will do this by calling for repentance. And Jesus is to be the Davidic King who will reign over Israel for ever. Mary has been identified not only as the mother of Jesus, but also as a model believer. The scene is set for the birth of both babies.

## THE STRUCTURE

| | |
|---|---|
| 1:39-45 | The Baptist's joy |
| 1:46-56 | Mary's praise at God's salvation |
| 1:57-66 | The Baptist's birth |
| 1:67-80 | Zechariah's prophecy of God's salvation |

## OLD TESTAMENT NOTES

*Hannah, mother of Samuel:* The Old Testament prophet Samuel prepared the way for King David. Samuel was born to a barren woman, Hannah. Hannah praised God for the birth of Samuel (1 Sam. 2). Most of the themes in Hannah's prayer – praise of God, God's holiness and majesty, God's rescue of His people, God's reversal of human values – will be found in Mary's prayer.

*'to Abraham and to his offspring':* In Genesis 12:1-2 and Genesis 15, God made promises to Abraham that are foundational to the whole Bible. Abraham was to be father to God's people, established in a place that God would give, and all the nations would experience God's blessing through Abraham. The fulfilment of this promise began with the miraculous birth of Isaac (Gen. 21).

*'his holy covenant':* God's promises to Abraham are known as His covenant. In Genesis 17:8, God promised to Abraham that, for his offspring, '... I will be their God.'

*'the sunrise shall visit us':* Malachi's prophecy (see Study 1) promised that on the day God visited His people '... the sun of righteousness shall rise with healing in its wings.' (Mal. 4:2).

*'light to those who sit in darkness':* In Isaiah 9:2 and 42:7, God promises that the coming of His King and the work of His Servant will bring light and liberty for those in darkness and captivity. In Isaiah's prophecy darkness, blindness and captivity refer to God's judgment on His people for their sin.

## TEXT NOTES

### 1:39-45 THE BAPTIST'S JOY

Mary has already been identified by Luke as providing a model response. Now Elizabeth affirms Mary's response; Mary is 'blessed' because she 'believed'. These verses, and those that follow, are filled with joy, praise, delight and blessing. Mary and Elizabeth both grasp the magnitude of what is taking place. So does John the Baptist! He is already leaping for joy in the womb in anticipation of Jesus' birth.

1:46-56 MARY'S PRAISE AT GOD'S SALVATION

Mary's joy produces an overflow of praise. Her poem is known as 'the Magnificat'. Her praise is both exemplary and instructive. The subject of her praise is God's salvation, and its context is all God's promises in the Old Testament.

*Mary as model*: Luke has already indicated that Mary is a model believer. Her prayer is God-centred, joyful, personal and humble. Her mind is steeped in Scripture – and it would appear that she has been meditating on 1 Samuel 2. The significance of this link to Hannah, whose own prayer came at a time when God was acting in a ground-breaking way to provide a rescuing king, should not be overlooked. God is praised for His holiness, majesty and strength. The joy in the prayer is also a characteristic of so many of the responses in the first two chapters of Luke (1:14, 42, 64; 2:10, 13, 20, 28). Mary prays to 'God my Saviour' (v. 47) and recognises that he 'has done great things for me' (v. 49); the prayer is intensely personal. Above all, the prayer is humble. Mary recognises her own personal need for salvation. There is no hint here, or anywhere else in the gospel, of Mary being sinless or perfect. She acknowledges her own need of a saviour and rejoices at her salvation.

*Mary's message*: The main theme of Mary's praise is God's power to rescue and to bring about a divine reversal. Her prayer is not just an example; it also provides instruction as to what God is doing. God's rescue is highlighted in the opening lines, in which many of the verbs are in the past tense. Mary is so confident that God will fulfil His promise that she can speak as if it has already happened. His rescue is underwritten by both His strength and His faithfulness. Because God's 'arm' (v. 51) is mighty and because God cannot renege on His promises, so the success of His action in mercy towards His people is guaranteed. He made promises to Abraham – now He is acting to fulfil them. In the same way, God's work of bringing about a divine reversal is in keeping with His character. He will scatter those who have puffed themselves up in their own self-importance, because He has always hated the proud and arrogant (Prov. 6:16-17), especially when their pride is manifested in a rejection of God. God has always promised favour to those who humble themselves before Him (Isa. 66:1-2).

Divine rescue and divine reversal are two of the great themes in this Gospel. They are closely connected: God reveals Himself to the humble (10:21), and exalts them (14:11); the Kingdom of God is only for the humble (18:17). Conversely, Jesus promises to bring down the proud (10:15), and pronounces woe on them (11:42); God hides Himself from the proud (10:21), and they are an abomination to Him (16:15). Humility, in Luke's Gospel, is evidenced by the recognition of the need for salvation and a willingness to receive Jesus as Saviour. Pride is evidenced by self-righteousness and the rejection of God's salvation. Humility and pride, in this Gospel, are linked to physical poverty and wealth – but they are *definitely* not synonymous with them. Verse 53 is a direct quotation from Psalm 107, confirming that 'the hungry' refers to the 'longing soul' and the 'hungry soul' (Ps. 107:9). Those 'of humble estate' (v. 52) are those who recognise their spiritual poverty. They may be poor or rich. Later in the Gospel we find a middle-class fisherman, the wife of a senior palace official, a rich tax collector, a once-wealthy heir, a senior military officer and a leading synagogue ruler, all evidencing this spiritual humility and hunger, in company with the leper, the prostitute, the labourer and the 'sinner'.

## 1:57-66 The Baptist's birth

The events surrounding the birth of the Baptist indicate that Zechariah has learned the lesson of his silence. The birth is marked by joy, fear, and thoughtful wonder. The choice of John's unusual name and Zechariah's sudden recovery both make an impact on the neighbours and relatives, causing fear, widespread discussion and thoughtful reflection. The testimony of verse 65 hints that Dr Luke interviewed at least some of those who were there at the time. Verse 66 is key. The phrase 'the hand of the Lord' is repeatedly used in the Old Testament to speak of God's power, particularly with reference to His saving work (Exod. 15:6; Isa. 31:3).

1:67-80 ZECHARIAH'S PROPHECY OF GOD'S SALVATION

As with Mary's prayer, the subject of Zechariah's prophecy is salvation (vv. 68, 69, 71, 74, 77, 78), and the past tense is used to indicate certain fulfilment. The prophecy is steeped in Old Testament references, showing that what has taken place is an accomplishment of God's plan (Luke 1:1; 24:44). Throughout the Gospel we learn that the Old Testament is the 'interpretative grid' through which we come to understand Jesus' work (1:1; 24:26-27; 24:44-47).

*vv67-75 Jesus and the goal of salvation:* Zechariah declares that God is at work in redemption (v. 68). His work is a work of mighty salvation (v. 69). A 'horn' in the Bible is used to indicate strength and power – after the power of the strongest beast, the ox (cf. 2 Sam. 22:3; Ps. 18:2). God's work is centred on His promise to David (v. 69). The heart of His work is salvation (v. 71). The grounds for His work is His covenant promise to Abraham (vv. 72-73). The goal of His work is that His people should serve Him confidently in holiness and righteousness (vv. 4-75). In this first part of his prophecy, Zechariah interprets to his listeners what has been going on. The primary focus is salvation through the long-promised Davidic King, in accordance with all God's promises. But salvation in the Bible is never an end in itself; it is always worked out in service. God saves His people for service (Exod. 7:16; 8:1, 20). He redeems for a reason.

*vv76-80 The Baptist and the essence of salvation:* Zechariah addresses his new-born baby with the language of Malachi 3:1. John's 'job description' – 'for you will go before the Lord to prepare his ways' – is, by now, familiar. Later this job description will be repeated by Jesus (7:27) and the job re-allocated to Jesus' disciples (9:52; 10:1). Verses 77-79 are immensely significant. With careful precision Zechariah defines for his audience the essence of this saving work of God. Forgiveness of sins lies at the centre of God's salvation. It is rooted in the merciful character of God (v. 78). The possibility of salvation comes through a divine visitation (see Old Testament Notes). Its result is light, life and peace. Throughout the Gospel Luke continually returns to the theme of peace (2:14; 7:50; 8:48; 19:38; 24:36). Here Zechariah defines the word for us: peace in Luke's Gospel is peace with God through the salvation that comes as sins are forgiven.

## Key Themes

The big theme of these verses is God's work of salvation. Jesus, the Son of God, has come as Saviour of His people:

- ✤ He has come as a mighty Saviour, whose strength will guarantee that He accomplishes God's salvation
- ✤ He has come to save, in fulfilment of God's great promises to Abraham and David
- ✤ His salvation will result in a great 'reversal' as the proud enemies of God are humbled and the humble are exalted
- ✤ His salvation has, at its heart, the forgiveness of sins that brings peace with God
- ✤ His salvation will result in His saved people serving God confidently in holiness and righteousness
- ✤ His saving work is rightly met with joy, praise, and delight

## Application

*To them then:* Luke's goal is that Theophilus should be certain. Luke wants his reader to grasp that God has indeed accomplished the salvation of His people. This salvation is guaranteed both by the promises of God and by the power of the Saviour. It has at its heart the forgiveness of sins which will bring peace with God, and lead to active service. This is no new-fangled idea. It is the climax of everything that God has been promising from the earliest days of Israel's existence. It is rooted in Old Testament promise, and worked out in publicly-witnessed historical events.

Most importantly, Mary, through her prayer, and Zechariah, through his authoritative instruction, interpret the events for Luke's reader. Theophilus is not left simply to 'make up his own mind' about what he is being told. The meaning is precisely tied down by the interpretative words of Zechariah. Peace with God, through the forgiveness of sins by God's long-promised Saviour, is what lies at the heart of salvation. The events Luke has recorded should produce joy, praise and delight. The darkness is about to be lifted and death will be defeated.

These verses also provide an explanation as to why some people will not recognise this salvation. It is the proud who will never accept it. God will humble them. But the humble will receive it with joy and thanksgiving. God will exalt them.

*To us now*: These verses should give us clarity and confidence. Just as in the first century, there are many in the twenty-first century who reject God's salvation. There are also many who would explain it in terms other than the forgiveness of sins that brings peace with God. They have other 'agendas' for Jesus than a Biblical one. This ought not to perturb us. We can have a deep confidence in the meaning of what is taking place because both Mary and Zechariah spell out God's interpretation of what is going on. Therefore, we should discard any explanation that does not locate itself in the context of the Old Testament promises and in Mary and Zechariah's interpretation of them.

We can also have confidence in the salvation itself. The events recorded are publicly witnessed and widely known. Nothing will stop this great plan of God. He is acting in Jesus to save His people by forgiving their sins. Forgiveness of sin lies at the heart of His salvation. It results in the blessings promised in the Old Testament: peace with God, defeat of death, and confident joyful service. God's purposes will be fulfilled because He has the power to accomplish them. Those who seek to impose on Jesus an alternative agenda of their own invention should beware. Through the work of Jesus, the Saviour, God is in the business of bringing down the proud. Humble recognition of our need will result in salvation.

## THE AIM

The aim of this study is to gain joyful confidence in the salvation that Jesus has come to bring.

## Suggested Initial Questions

- ⚘ Introduction
    - ↘ Summarise the message of the angel to Zechariah (1:13-17) and to Mary (1:30-33).
    - ↘ In what way is Mary shown to be a model believer (1:38)?
- ⚘ 1:39-45
    - ↘ How do the words and emotions in verses 39-45 underscore what Luke taught us in 1:5-38?
- ⚘ 1:46-56
    - ↘ What are the key themes of Mary's prayer?
    - ↘ How does Mary's use of Hannah's song in 1 Samuel 2 clarify what God is doing and how he is doing it?
    - ↘ What do these themes teach us about God?
    - ↘ What do these themes teach us about who, and how, God will bless?
- ⚘ 1:57-66
    - ↘ Zechariah's obedience to the angel's command (1:63) results in his mouth being opened. What is the impact of his ability to speak returning? How does this give us confidence?
- ⚘ 1:67-80
    - ↘ Zechariah's prophecy is all about God's salvation. In what ways do we see that?
    - ↘ Verses 76-77 define the precise nature of the salvation that the Most High will bring. What is it? What will it result in (vv. 78-79)?
    - ↘ Mary's praise and Zechariah's prophecy are both steeped in the Old Testament. And in both cases the salvation that Jesus has come to bring is spoken of in the past tense. What do these two things achieve?
- ⚘ Summary
    - ↘ How does what we have learned give us confidence concerning the content of the Gospel, and also its credibility?

# The Birth of the Saviour
## Luke 2:1-21

## THE CONTEXT

Luke's aim is that his reader, Theophilus, should be clear and certain about the content of the gospel ('the things that have been accomplished among us' 1:1-4). This will lead to a commitment to the gospel's global advance (24:44-47). Luke's material has been gleaned from authorised eyewitnesses. In chapter 1 he has already demonstrated historical precision; His detailed accounts of the testimony of various individuals give the reader confidence that what he is recording really did happen. This theme of historical accuracy and eyewitness testimony continues throughout this study. Luke's account informs us not only about what took place, but also about its meaning. Mary declares that the King from the line of David is 'my Saviour'. Zechariah's prophecy describes this 'salvation' in terms of 'the forgiveness of sins' and 'peace'. All of this is in line with the great promises of God to His people. There is, then, no departure from all that God 'spoke to our fathers, to Abraham and to his offspring for ever' (1:55), for God has remembered 'his holy covenant, the oath that he swore to our father Abraham' (1:72-73).

## THE STRUCTURE

**2:1-8**     The facts of Jesus' birth
**2:9-14**    The meaning of Jesus' birth
**2:15-21**   The verification of Jesus' birth

## OLD TESTAMENT NOTES

*'the city of David'*: Jerusalem is frequently referred to as David's city, for Jerusalem is the city that David chose and built up as the capital of Israel. It was the site of the temple and therefore the centre of all God's dealings with His historic people. David's father, Jesse, and his grandfather, Obed, both came from the tribe of Judah, and Bethlehem was their home town (1 Sam. 16:18; Ruth 1:2; 4:1).

## TEXT NOTES

### 2:1-8 THE FACTS OF JESUS' BIRTH

*The birth is historical:* Dr Luke's concern for precise historical detail is again evident in these verses. The events of Jesus' birth take place against a backcloth of verifiable global history. Luke wants us to know that we are dealing in reality, not myth. Caesar Augustus (also known as Octavian) was emperor of Rome from 27 B.C. to A.D. 14. He was responsible for introducing imperial taxes into the Roman system. Quirinius was governor of Syria in A.D. 6 and Herod the Great (1:5) was king of Judea from 37-4 B.C. This presents two problems with the dating surrounding Jesus' birth. How could Jesus have been born during the reign of Herod the Great in A.D. 1 if Herod the Great died in 4 B.C.? And how could Mary and Joseph be travelling to Bethlehem on account of Quirinius' census if Quirinius did not become governor until A.D. 6?

Both issues can be explained without compromising Luke's account. First, the B.C. / A.D. calendar was produced by a monk named Dionysius. He was tasked to reform the Roman calendar along Christian lines, making Jesus' birth central. It is well documented that he miscalculated the death of Herod and that the B.C./ A.D. calendar is 'out' by at least 4–6 years. It is most likely that Jesus was born in about 6 B.C. This makes the second issue (Quirinius' census) even more problematic. He became governor of Syria in A.D. 6, so how could Mary and Joseph be taking part in his census in 6 B.C.? This 'problem' is significantly reduced when one considers the length of time that is required to compile a census. The UK census of 2013 took well over eighteen months to complete, with all the modern communication technology. The census of Gaul, taken just before the Judean census, took forty years to complete. Quirinius was a senior Roman official in the region of Syria for some time prior to his promotion to governor. It is perfectly reasonable to suppose that Quirinius or another official commissioned the census at least a decade prior to its completion – probably more.

*The birth is royal*: Verses 4-5 remind us that we are dealing with royalty (see chapter 1 and Old Testament Notes). God promised David that his throne would be established 'for ever' (2 Sam. 7:16; Isa. 9:6-7). This promise was picked up by the prophet Micah, who announced that 'one who is to be ruler in Israel, whose origin is from of old' would come from 'Bethlehem, Ephrathah' (Micah 5:2). The promise of the angel (1:32, 35) is fulfilled in 2:4-6. This is a royal birth, the birth of God's eternal king, who was to be given 'the throne of his father David, and he will reign over the house of Jacob for ever, and of his kingdom there will be no end.' (1:32-33)

*The birth is humble*: It is also a humble birth. This infant, though rich beyond all splendour, became poor. God entered the world in human form, but with a characteristic lack of pomp and pageantry. The scandal of the incarnation anticipates the sacrifice of the crucifixion; there is a consistent trajectory from the manger to the cross. Jesus came in selfless humility.

2:8-14 THE MEANING OF JESUS' BIRTH

*vv8-9*: The appearance of the glory of the Lord is very rare in the Bible. It happened at Mount Sinai (Exod. 19), when Solomon dedicated the newly-built Temple (1 Kings 8), and when Isaiah had his vision (Isa. 6), but it is a rarity. Always it produced fear in God's people, even as it accompanied His great acts and announcements. Luke's emphasis is not, however, on the shepherds' experience of the glory of God, but on the explanatory statement. Once again Dr

Luke records the authentic interpretation. There are two parts to the explanation.

*vv10-11 The rescue:* Joy, thanksgiving and praise permeate these chapters. It is 'good news of great joy' (v. 10), Simeon 'took him up in his arms and blessed God' (v. 28), and Anna 'began to give thanks to God' (v. 38). The reason for this outpouring is stated in verse 11. Twice the angel stresses the royalty and divinity of the child: He is born in 'the city of David' (see Old Testament Notes), and He is 'Christ the Lord'. This is a divine, royal child. Between the statements about royal origin and divine rule comes a statement about the purpose of the child's birth – He is 'a Saviour'. We have already noted this emphasis on Jesus' mission (1:47, 54, 69-77). Now the divine royal Ruler is identified as the Saviour from God. This is the heart of the 'good news of a great joy that will be for all the people.' (v. 10)

*vv13-14 The reconciliation:* The proclamation from the angelic choir explains the nature of the rescue that is to be accomplished. We have already learned from Zechariah that 'peace' is rooted in 'salvation' and that this 'salvation' involves 'the forgiveness of their sins.' (1:77-79) This rescue from God is set to accomplish reconciliation between God and humanity. (To follow up on this theme in Luke's Gospel, see 7:48-50; 8:48; 19:9-10, 23-39).

2:15-21 THE VERIFICATION OF JESUS' BIRTH

*vv15-21:* Commentators like to write about the social status of shepherds in first-century Palestine. Luke makes no mention of this, and we should avoid speculation. What Luke does stress is the presence of eyewitnesses at this event, the explanatory word, and the appropriate response.

*The eyewitnesses:* That the shepherds are eyewitnesses is underlined both at the beginning and at the end of the paragraph: 'Let us go over to Bethlehem and see' (v. 15), and 'the shepherds returned, glorifying and praising God for all they had heard and seen, as it had been told them' (v. 20). We are dealing here with eyewitness testimony.

*The explanatory word:* The English translations of this passage obscure the point that Luke wants us to grasp. The same Greek word is translated in verse 15 as 'this thing', in verse 17 as 'the saying', and in verse 19 as 'these things'; it can be translated as either 'saying' or 'thing'. The shepherds go to Bethlehem to verify 'the saying' of the angels. They make known this 'saying', and Mary then treasures up 'all these things', or 'sayings', 'pondering them in her heart'. The emphasis is on the facts as they happen and the meaning attributed to them by the 'saying' of the angel. Jesus is the royal Saviour from God and He has been born just as God's angel said. We are dealing here with historical events, but they are historical events with God-given meaning and purpose.

*The appropriate response:* The shepherds overflow with praise to God. God's long-awaited rescuer, the Davidic King, who had been promised throughout the Old Testament, has finally arrived. This is the good news of great joy for all the people. The word 'ponder' is a word used for 'conferring' or 'throwing things together'. Mary treasures up all the sayings concerning the baby and confers within herself about them. This implies careful thought and consideration. Once again she provides the model.

## Key Themes

*Historical precision:* Dr Luke wants us to have confidence in his historical record, based on eyewitness accounts. The text is full of historical detail and personal testimony.

*The God-given meaning of what has happened:*
- the baby is the long-promised Davidic Messiah
- the baby is the God-given Saviour who will bring divine reconciliation and, thereby, peace

*The proper response:* the two elements of this feed each other:
- joy, wonder and praise
- careful meditation

## Application

*To them then:* Luke wants Theophilus to be in no doubt concerning the facts of what has happened, the importance of these facts, and their meaning. This ties in with what we have seen already, in the opening words of the Gospel: Luke's aim is that his reader should be certain concerning the things that have taken place. He wants his reader to grasp not only the detail of the Gospel events, but also their meaning – the theological content of the gospel. Once again the meaning is rooted precisely in the Old Testament context. To understand this child rightly requires a grasp of the Old Testament word of God. This is far more important than the emphasis some might place on inter-Testamental writings, or first-century archaeology. God had promised a Saviour who was to be the Christ – a divine rescuer. As the sky over Bethlehem is filled with the spectacular appearance of the angels – 'a multitude of the heavenly host praising God' – their words proclaim in the most powerful way that these promises are now being fulfilled. The shepherds discover that the angels' words were true, that what had been announced had indeed taken place, and this should encourage Theophilus, like Mary, to think long and hard about the precise detail of the announcement. Reading the account of this amazing divine intervention, recorded in verses 10-14, will encourage him to ponder the meaning of the rescue and also the identity of the rescuer.

*To us now*: We will do well to note the careful historical detail in verses 1-7. This should strengthen our confidence in Dr Luke's account, and thereby strengthen our confidence concerning the reality of what has happened in history. God has broken in from outside. He has come in fulfilment of all His promises. True to His revealed character, He has come in selfless humility. This humble birth sets the trajectory for the kingly ministry of Jesus throughout the gospel – and for the life of His disciples. Divine reversal of this sort becomes the 'normal' in the gospel. However, the thrust of these verses drives us to consider the meaning of what has happened. The long-promised king has come as God from God to rescue. Luke will not allow us to think of Jesus as simply a great moral teacher, urging us to pull our socks up, or a mighty miracle worker, or a supreme social reformer, urging us to engage in societal reform. Christianity is first and foremost a rescue religion, because Christ has come as a saviour to bring peace between God and humanity. This is the good news of great joy for all the people. We should share the joy of the angels and the shepherds.

This joy will come as we emulate Mary in her careful consideration of all the sayings concerning the Lord Jesus.

## The Aim

The aim of this study is that we should reflect joyfully on the identity of Jesus, and on the purpose of His coming.

## Suggested Initial Questions

- ✤ Introduction
  - ↘ What did we learn from Mary's prayer and Zechariah's prophecy about the purpose of Jesus' coming into the world?
- ✤ 2:1-7
  - ↘ Luke includes a large number of historical details. How does this help to build confidence in his account? *(Be prepared for questions on Quirinius and Augustus – see Text Notes.)*
  - ↘ How does the description of Jesus' birth pick up on the themes to be found in Mary's prayer and Zechariah's prophecy?
- ✤ 2:8-14
  - ↘ Appearances of God and of His angels are extremely rare in the Bible. What are the key themes in the angels' words (vv. 10-12 and 14)?
  - ↘ How do these themes help explain the different emotions that we find spoken of and expressed in verses 8-14?
- ✤ 2:15-21
  - ↘ In what ways does Luke's record of the shepherds' actions serve to build confidence in what the angels have said?
  - ↘ How do the responses of the shepherds and of Mary provide us with a model?
- ✤ Summary
  - ↘ What causes for confident joy and hope have we been given in this study?

# The Saviour of the World
## Luke 2:22-52

## The Context

The narrative of Luke's account began at the temple with the announcement of the Baptist's birth. From the beginning of his narrative Luke has introduced the following key concepts:

*History:* This is eyewitness testimony, embedded in national and international history.

*Fulfilment:* Old Testament promise is being fulfilled. Also, it is providing the 'interpretative grid' by which the events are to be understood.

*Identity:* Jesus is identified as the divine Davidic ruler.

*Mission:* Jesus has come as Saviour to bring salvation (peace with God) through the forgiveness of sins.

*Explanation:* The 'words' or sayings of prophecy, of angelic revelation, and of Old Testament Scripture make sense of what is taking place.

*Response:* These words are to be carefully received and considered.

Luke now takes his reader back to the temple, the centre of God's relationship with His historic people, Israel. The baby Jesus is welcomed into the temple. He is introduced as the redeeming figure towards whom the whole temple, with its Law and sacrificial system, was pointing. The twelve-year-old Jesus then explains Himself as the divine Son who is in His father's house and who has to be about His father's business.

## THE STRUCTURE

**2:22-40**    This baby is God's Saviour for the nations
**2:41-52**    This child is God's Son, going about His Father's work of salvation

## OLD TESTAMENT NOTES

*The dedication of the first-born:* The Passover (Exod. 12) was the foundational act of God in the Old Testament, when He rescued (redeemed) His people from slavery in Egypt. The people of God were rescued at the same time that God brought judgment on His enemies. God's people escaped judgment through the death of a lamb in the place of each first-born son. From that point on every first-born son had to be redeemed by a sacrifice in the temple. This was designed to remind God's people that they were a rescued people, belonging to the God who redeems (Exod. 13:2, 13:11-14; Num. 3:11-13). Mary and Joseph's sacrifice at the temple was part of this ritual reminder (Lev. 12:2-8).

'*the consolation of Israel*': God's historic people, Israel, were taken captive from the land of Israel as a result of their sinful rebellion against God. It was God's just punishment on them for their sin. This captivity is known as 'the Exile'. God promised to bring an end to the Exile (Isa. 40:1-2). The end would come as God brought 'comfort' or 'consolation' to His people. He promised to provide 'a double' (an exact match) to cover His people's sins.[1] This provision of a sin-covering double would result in the ending of God's hostile anger towards His sinful people. Her warfare with God would

---

1. Alec Motyer writes: 'double is a dualised form of the noun ... meaning 'to fold double' ... the dual usage suggests two halves of something folded together in half, the one a replica of the other ... this points to a meaning like 'the equivalent' or 'that which exactly matches''. Revd Dr Alec Motyer, *The Prophecy of Isaiah*, (Leicester, England: IVP 1993), p. 299

be ended as her iniquity was pardoned. The comfort would come through an afflicted, sin-bearing servant, described in Isaiah 53.

*'a light for revelation to the Gentiles'*: The servant promised by God through Isaiah was to have a mission that would extend far beyond the borders of Israel. God promised to send a servant who would be 'a light for the nations' (Isa. 42:6). The purpose of this servant's ministry would be that God's 'salvation may reach to the end of the earth' (Isa. 49:6), and that 'all the ends of the earth shall see the salvation of our God' (Isa. 52:10).

*The temple:* The temple was key to God's dwelling among His people. It was the place of sacrifice. The sacrificial system was the means by which God's people remained in a right relationship with Him. The temple was also the place of revelation. The priests taught God's people in the temple. Above all, the temple was the place where God dwelt among His people in all holiness and purity. It was 'God's house'; 'God's dwelling place on earth'.

*'the redemption of Jerusalem'*: God's rescue of His people from exile (see above) included a promise of restoration of the city of Jerusalem. This city is often referred to as Zion. Promises concerning Zion can be found in Isaiah 60 and 62. God speaks of setting 'watchmen' on 'the walls of Jerusalem' (Isa. 62:6). These watchmen wait for the redemption of Jerusalem.

## TEXT NOTES

### 2:22-40 THIS BABY IS GOD'S SAVIOUR FOR THE NATIONS

This section works like a sandwich, with the 'meat', the main point, in the middle. It begins and ends with a reminder of the requirements of the Law of the Lord for any first-born son in Israel (vv. 22-24 and 39-40). Then Simeon and Anna are introduced, and both draw attention to the rescue that Jesus will accomplish (vv. 25-28 and 36-38). The main point of this passage, the explanation, is in the words spoken by Simeon, first to God in praise and then to Mary and Joseph in prophecy (vv. 29-35).

*vv22-24 The Law and God's salvation:* Luke's narrative now returns to the temple. The Law required that for every firstborn male sacrifices should be made on his behalf (see Old Testament Notes). Luke's purpose in recording Mary and Joseph's obedience to the Law is not that his readers should focus on this, but rather that they should be reminded once again of God's specific purpose, to rescue His people and make them a holy nation dedicated to Himself. It is in this context that Simeon and Anna rejoice, and that Simeon speaks his words of prophecy.

*vv25-28 Simeon and God's Saviour:* 'Righteous and devout', Simeon was waiting for the Christ and for 'the consolation' (or 'comfort', same word) of God's people (see Old Testament Notes). As Mary and Joseph come 'to do for him according to the custom of the Law', Simeon takes the child in his arms and, like Zechariah before him, is filled with the Holy Spirit as he blesses God and provides the interpretation of these events. Throughout these verses the emphasis is on God's promised salvation and Saviour.

*vv29-35 The promise of God's salvation,* 'a light ... to the Gentiles': Luke is determined that his readers should grasp the content of the gospel message. He directs their attention to the explanatory word that has already come from God. The phrase 'your word' in verse 29 uses the same Greek word that is found in 2:15, 17 and 19, and also in 2:50 and 51. It is God's word of revelation that makes sense of the extraordinary events being recorded. Again, the mission of Jesus as Saviour is stressed; Simeon has seen the 'salvation' that has come from God, and now he can depart 'in peace'. This time, however, the emphasis is on the scope of this salvation. God's promise that His salvation was to be 'for the nations' would be fulfilled in Jesus (see Old Testament Notes).

'for the fall and rising of many': Verses 33-35 strike a sombre note. Simeon's words to Mary and Joseph indicate that Jesus will cause some to rise and others to fall – He will judge even as He saves. Mary has already spoken of this (1:52) – the Lord has 'brought down the mighty' and 'exalted those of humble estate'. This great reversing work of God is to be accomplished through the revealing, rescuing work of Jesus. He will be opposed, and the opposition will cause Mary's heart to be pierced also. This prophecy by Simeon anticipates the divisive nature of Jesus' mission which will be hated by so many, and which will take Him, ultimately, to the cross.

*vv36-38 Anna and God's Saviour:* Eighty-four-year-old Anna, like Simeon in verses 25-28, is awaiting the redemption of Jerusalem. Luke characteristically records precise details of Anna's age, marital status, family background, and role. The detail of verses 36 and 37 removes Luke's account absolutely from the literary genre of myth or legend. At the same time the verses re-emphasise the mission of Jesus. He has come to a people awaiting rescue. And Anna can be seen as a watchman, prayerfully longing for the redemption of Jerusalem (see Old Testament Notes). Her praise signals the end of the people's waiting.

*vv39-40 The Law and God's salvation:* The Law of the Lord, with its inherent testimony to God's salvation, serves its purpose absolutely as it is fulfilled in Jesus' presentation at the temple. Verse 40 is reminiscent of 1 Samuel 2:21 and 26, and is intended as a reminder of a previous occasion when God rescued His people through the provision of a redeeming king, David.

*2:41-52 THIS CHILD IS GOD'S SON GOING ABOUT HIS FATHER'S WORK OF SALVATION*

*Identity:* Whether it is God's work or God's temple to which Jesus refers, by calling God 'my Father' He is speaking words that no other devout Jew would have dared to use. 'This child was conscious of a relationship with God that none had conceived let alone expressed before'[2]. Jesus is voicing here what had been heralded by the angels. The point is emphasised by the fact that He says 'the saying' to Mary and Joseph – Joseph is His earthly parent, God is His true father. On the lips of a twelve-year-old boy, in the temple, this is either unequalled precocious arrogance or, if true, an announcement as unique as it is explosive. This is called by some the 'high point' of the infancy narrative. It is not hard to understand why. Jesus is personally introducing Himself, at the age of twelve, as God the Son, the Son of God.

*Mission:* Jesus is found in the temple in discussion with the 'teachers'. The setting of the temple, the context of the Passover and the careful use of the word 'must' all suggest that the young Jesus is already conscious of

---

2.    David Gooding, *According to Luke*, (Leicester, England: IVP 1987), p. 61

His mission to save. The temple was the place of revelation and sacrifice, and the Passover festival was a celebration of God's rescue (see Old Testament Notes). Luke uses the word 'must' only rarely in the Gospel, and it regularly speaks of the necessity of the cross (9:22; 22:37; 24:7, 26, 44). Jesus insists to His parents that He must be about the things of His Father. The rest of the Gospel and all of Scripture will demand that this business is accomplished at the cross.

*Response:* Throughout the first two chapters, Luke has drawn attention to what is the right response to God's word (1:45, 66; 2:19). Here we find him emphasising a different response: Mary and Joseph 'did not understand the saying'. This inability to grasp fully what is being said is a regular feature in the gospel (9:45; 18:34). Eventually human blindness is remedied as the risen Jesus instructs His disciples from the written word of God (24:27, 31-32, 45).

## KEY THEMES

*Salvation:* The emphasis on the mission of Jesus as Saviour continues. In this study fresh dimensions are introduced. He is God's Saviour, not just for Israel but for all nations. The salvation He has come to bring will result in judgment as well as rescue.

*Identity:* At the 'high point' of the narrative the twelve-year-old Jesus introduces Himself. He is God the Son, the Son of God.

*Fulfilment:* The interpretation of these events is, as before, rooted in the Old Testament context. Luke is intent on demonstrating to his reader 'the things that have been accomplished among us' (1:1).

*Response:* Like Mary, the reader is to treasure up these 'sayings' in the heart.

## APPLICATION

*To them then:* These verses, more than any earlier part of Luke's narrative, assemble Old Testament ideas, in order to emphasise that Jesus has come as God's Saviour. Simeon and Anna point to this. So do Mary and Joseph, as they bring Jesus, the first-born, to the temple to present Him in a ceremony prescribed by the Law, a ceremony that reminded everyone of the Passover, and God's intention of redeeming a people for Himself. Most importantly, Simeon's words point to Jesus' role in securing salvation for the nations as well as for God's people, Israel. This salvation is the ending of hostility between God and humanity, as Luke indicates by mentioning that Simeon was 'waiting for the consolation of Israel'. The first reader of this Gospel would have recalled Isaiah's prophecy about this, that forgiveness of sins would bring an end to the hostility. Luke wants his reader to grasp that the birth of Jesus means that the Saviour of the world has arrived. The presentation of the baby Jesus in the temple is matched by the twelve-year-old Jesus' introduction of Himself in the temple. He declares Himself to be the Son of the Father, who must make His Father's business – namely, salvation – His own. Throughout this passage, Luke encourages his reader to gather up all the verbal sayings concerning Jesus, and to think about them.

*To us now:* Some modern commentaries are full of suggestions that Luke is pursuing his own particular agenda, and wants to present Jesus in the light of his own understanding of salvation. We need to recognise, however, that Luke has no agenda, other than to show us that all God's promises in the Old Testament, concerning a divine, sin-bearing Saviour for all nations, have been fulfilled in the arrival of Jesus. Luke's emphasis on the 'sayings', in these early chapters, repeatedly directs us to the words spoken by Zechariah, Simeon, Anna and others, as the Holy Spirit revealed the truth to them, and the words of Jesus Himself. All these 'sayings' emphasise that Jesus has come as the Saviour of the world. This study should fill us with confidence as we learn the details of Jesus' identity and mission: the Law is fulfilled in Jesus, the temple points to Jesus, the prophets spoke of Jesus, Jesus is the Saviour of the world, Jesus is the Son of God, Jesus is God the Son.

## THE AIM

The aim of this study is to see that Jesus has come as the Saviour of the world.

## SUGGESTED INITIAL QUESTIONS

✤ Introduction

↘ Summarise the message of the angels in 2:10-12 and 2:14.

↘ What did we learn from the shepherds' action and from Mary's response in 2:15-21?

✣ 2:22-40

↘ Read Isaiah 40:1-2. What was it that God promised to His people in these verses?

↘ Read Isaiah 49:6-7. How do these verses extend the promise of Isaiah 40:1-2?

↘ Read Luke 2:22-40. How do the Isaiah passages help us make sense of what Simeon and Anna are both waiting for?

↘ Re-read Luke 2:29-32. Why does Simeon think that he is now ready to die 'in peace'?

↘ What five things do Simeon's words to Mary and Joseph (vv. 33-35) suggest will happen as a result of this baby's life?

↘ The events in these verses take place in the temple, on account of Mary and Joseph abiding by the Jewish Law. What is the significance of this?

✣ 2:41-52

↘ What are the implications of the way Jesus speaks of God and of the temple (in v. 49) for (a) His identity and (b) His mission?

↘ How does what Jesus says in verse 49 help to explain the events of verses 41-48?

↘ All this takes place at the time of Passover as the people of Israel remember God's act of redemption (Exod. 12). What is the significance of Jesus' words, spoken in this context, and of His leaving His parents (v. 49)? What do we learn from Mary's response (vv. 50-51)?

↘ Why is it important that Luke wrote verses 39-40 and 52?

✣ Summary

↘ How has this study helped to clarify, and create confidence in, Jesus' identity and mission?

# Preparing for the Saviour
## Luke 3:1-20

## THE CONTEXT

In the first chapter of Luke's account, the birth of John the Baptist and his future ministry are prominent. John's father, Zechariah, has explained the Baptist's ministry: he is to 'go before the Lord to prepare his ways'; he is to 'give knowledge of salvation' to the people 'in the forgiveness of their sins'. Having recorded and explained the birth of the Baptist and of Jesus, Luke now turns to the public ministry of John the Baptist. Once again Luke organises his material to achieve his stated goals. First, the gospel is being defined, as John proclaims 'a baptism of repentance for the forgiveness of sins' (v. 3) – this *is* the gospel. The Baptist's ministry is gospel work – 'he preached good news' (v. 18). Then, the gospel is being defended, as Luke locates John's ministry both in its first-century historical setting and in its Old Testament context. By defining the gospel, and defending it, Luke prepares the reader to understand the gospel when it is declared. This study should build our confidence in the content of the gospel and its credibility, and also about the need to communicate it to the world.

## THE STRUCTURE

**3:1-14**     The Baptist's message: proclaiming a baptism of repentance for the forgiveness of sins

**3:15-20**    The Baptist's ministry: preaching the good news of Jesus Christ

## OLD TESTAMENT NOTES

*The voice:* In Isaiah 40 a fresh start is promised for God's people after the Exile (see Old Testament Notes for Study 4). This fresh start is to be heralded by 'a voice'. The voice will cry out, 'In the wilderness prepare the way of the Lord'. The voice, with its summons to make preparation, will be followed by the dramatic intervention of God Himself (Isa. 40:3-5).

'*We have Abraham as our father*': God's promises to Abraham are the foundation of the nation of Israel's relationship with God. Abraham was called by God, and God then made promises to Abraham: 'And I will make of you a great nation, and I will bless you and make your name great' (Gen. 12:2). Abraham's descendants were to be a great people, inheriting a great place (the land of Israel) and enjoying all God's great blessings, through His presence with them. Abraham was the father of Isaac and the grandfather of Jacob. The twelve tribes of Israel were descended from Jacob's twelve sons.

'*He will baptise you with the Holy Spirit*': The prophet Ezekiel recognised the failure of God's historic people, Israel, to live in faithful commitment to God. God promised a day when He would give His people new hearts by the work of His Holy Spirit within His people (Ezek. 36:26-27).

'*His winnowing fork is in his hand*': The Old Testament uses the images of a refiner's fire and of the separation of wheat from chaff at harvest to speak of God's coming judgment. The last book of the Old Testament speaks of the need to turn back to God in repentance in anticipation of His coming judgment (Mal. 3:2; 4:1).

## TEXT NOTES

3:1-14 THE BAPTIST'S MESSAGE: PROCLAIMING A BAPTISM OF REPENTANCE FOR THE FORGIVENESS OF SINS:

Luke summarises the work of John the Baptist in verse 3. Baptism involved immersion in water, but the rite itself was not the essence of the Baptist's ministry. Repentance translates a word which means 'a change of mind'. The Baptist was summoning people to change their minds and turn back to God. The initiative lies with God, for He is the one who commands repentance. The act of repentance is met by the offer of forgiveness, as John's father, Zechariah, had prophesied (1:77). Luke's opening summary of John's work in verse 3 is matched by the conclusion in verse 18. These two statements act as brackets and underline vital elements of true gospel proclamation, namely, the summons to repent, and the offer of forgiveness in Jesus' name.

*vv1-2 The historical background:* Characteristically, Luke provides historical detail. Tiberius Caesar governed the Roman Empire from A.D. 14–36. Pontius Pilate was governor of Israel A.D. 26–36. Herod and Philip were two of the three sons of the Jewish King Herod the Great (see 1:5). Philip ruled the North East (Iturea and Trachonitis) 4 B.C. – A.D. 34, and Herod the Tetrarch ruled Judea 4 B.C. – A.D. 39. We know little of Lysanias. Annas was High Priest A.D. 6–15, and his five sons succeeded him. Caiaphas was his son-in-law but Annas was still a very substantial 'presence'. Once again, Dr Luke's historical precision differentiates this material absolutely from myth, legend, or odyssey.

*vv4-6 The Baptist's biblical context:* Luke interprets John's ministry for the reader with reference to God's prior revelation in Isaiah 40 (see Old Testament notes). God Himself is about to intervene in history. His intervention will make salvation available for all people (cf. 2:29-32). The filling of valleys and levelling of hills refers to the ancient practice of constructing processional highways for victorious kings and generals. God is about to visit His people and bring His long-promised salvation for the world. Prepare the way! Make straight paths!

*vv7-9 Repentance must be personal:* The 'therefore' of verse 7 links the Baptist's message tightly to the prophecy of Isaiah that Luke has just quoted. The straight path and levelled highway along which the Lord will come with His salvation is one of personal repentance. Baptism itself was a public but highly personal act, indicating a profound change of mind. So the Baptist does not pull his punches: he warns of God's unavoidable coming judgment, and demands changed attitudes that will be worked out in action (v. 8). He warns his listeners not to presume on their inherited spiritual status. The Jews' connection with Abraham made them a highly privileged people (see Old Testament Notes), but there is no room for complacency. God is not interested in second-hand spiritual experience, and His blessings do not come automatically. He is perfectly able to make good His promise, to make a people for Himself, without the Jews – or us. Part of the Baptist's 'gospel' is to warn of God's judgment on all who fail to bear the fruit of genuine repentance, regardless of spiritual pedigree. Verses 16 and 17 warn that judgment will come, ultimately, at the hand of Jesus.

*vv10-14 Repentance must be radical:* Throughout Luke's Gospel, and also the book of Acts, the preaching of repentance is presented as an essential part of the gospel message (Luke 5:32; 15:7, 10; 19:1-10; 24:45-47; Acts 2:38; 5:31; 11:18). Even as forgiveness of sins is offered, repentance is demanded. If the 'change of mind' is to carry any weight with God, there must be a corresponding change in action – there is to be no 'cheap grace'. For *the crowd*, repentance would mean an end to greed and the start of a new generosity. Turning back to God, the giver of all good things, is to result in the growth of a family likeness (or 'fruit', v. 9) in His people as they become generous.

*Tax collectors* were a despised group. The occupying Romans sold them the franchise for collecting taxes on goods and services, and they then made their profit by adding their own 'cut' to the regulated tax. They were hated, therefore, both because they worked for the Romans and for their extortionate greed. Repentance for them would mean a wholesale change in business practice. Straight dealing, integrity and fair play were to become the hallmarks of those who turned back to the faithful and just God of Israel.

The text of verse 14 indicates that *the soldiers* (probably the local Jewish militia) were in the habit of using their powers for personal gain. For these government officials, also, repentance was to result in a new way of working. These three examples - a personal life of generosity and grace, a business life of integrity and fair play, and the exercise of responsibility and power without an eye to illicit personal gain - all indicate that the repentance sought by God is not simply an intellectual assent to theoretical propositions. It goes much deeper, and extends to practical submission to His Lordship over all of life. Baptism, together with this proclamation of 'repentance for the forgiveness of sins', raises the people's hopes. In verses 15-18 the Baptist clarifies his part in what is taking place, as he declares: 'but he who is mightier than I is coming'.

### 3:15-20 THE BAPTIST'S MINISTRY: PREACHING THE GOOD NEWS OF JESUS CHRIST

The angel Gabriel (1:16-17) and also Zechariah (1:76) had both explained that John the Baptist was to 'go before the Lord' as an Elijah figure, 'to make ready for the Lord a people prepared.' He was 'the warm-up act'. John is clear about his role (v. 16). As the angel had done when speaking to Zechariah, John refers to the prophecy of Malachi in order to describe his work. He is preparing for one far greater than himself (v. 16). This great one is Jesus, the judging Lord of Malachi 3:2 and 4:1 (see Old Testament Notes). He will bring the life-giving Spirit, as foretold in Ezekiel 36 (see Old Testament Notes). The Baptist (and baptism generally) is able to do no more than make a person wet, but the coming Lord Jesus will accomplish everything that baptism symbolises. He will flood a person's life with the presence of God the Holy Spirit; 'He will baptise you with the Holy Spirit and fire.' This is Bible shorthand for God's work of bringing new life (regeneration) as described in Ezekiel 36 and 37. Jesus' baptism will bring a new heart, with fresh desires and a new power to live for God. The 'fire' mentioned in verse 17 anticipates Jesus' role as judge.

Verse 18 provides a closing bracket to Luke's description of the Baptist's ministry (see v. 3). The summary of his work is: 'he preached good news'. This phrase 'preached good news' translates just one word from the original Greek – 'evangelised'. To 'evangelise' is the verb from the noun 'evangel', or 'gospel'. An 'evangel' or a 'gospel' is literally 'an announcement'. We have no verb 'to gospel' in the English language, but if we did verse 18 would be translated 'with many other exhortations he gospelled the people'. For John the Baptist, what then is the gospel? It is the announcement of nothing less than the arrival of Jesus as God's Lord and Judge, with the corresponding demand for repentance and the offer of forgiveness of sins to all who repent. New life is made possible through Jesus' coming: He will flood His people's hearts with His Holy Spirit. But judgment is certain for those who reject Jesus' offer.

The response of King Herod to the Baptist's ministry is precisely the response that Simeon foresaw as he held the baby Jesus in his arms (2:34). The gospel, with its demand for personal repentance and its warning of coming judgment, will be opposed; and opposition will prove costly for those who herald the Good News.

## KEY THEMES

*Repentance for the forgiveness of sins:* A personal, deep-rooted change of mind that leads to a changed life is fundamental to receiving God's offer of forgiveness of sins. Without this God-given response there can be no salvation.

*The gospel:* The gospel is the announcement of the coming of the Lord Jesus, who brings new life for His people and eternal punishment for those who refuse to repent.

## APPLICATION

*To them then:* Luke wants Theophilus to grasp that God's Saviour has broken into real human history in a particular place and at a particular time. The Saviour is not unexpected; He has been long promised. The salvation He brings is available for all people everywhere. However, this salvation from God demands a particular response, a response of deep-rooted, personal repentance towards

God. There is no 'cheap grace'. Furthermore, God is prepared to act in radical judgement on His historic people who have, in their complacency, shown no evidence of genuine concern for God and His character. Vast numbers of God's historic people will take this course, as will Herod. God will therefore raise up children for Himself from the nations. God can quite easily fulfil His plans for raising up a privileged people without His historic people Israel. He is not reliant on them. Inherited spiritual privileges count for nothing. The demand for a genuine response to God in repentance and faith is a fundamental part of the gospel, and is found in both Luke and Acts. It is a gospel of repentance for the forgiveness of sins. Repentance is to be far-reaching, impacting home life, business life and roles and responsibilities in society. The mighty Jesus, for whose coming John the Baptist urges people to prepare, is both Saviour and Judge. He is the one who can bring the in-flooding of the Holy Spirit and thus, by bringing new life, make possible the radical repentance of which John preaches. John's baptism merely points the way towards this – Jesus brings its reality. The refusal to repent and the rejection of Christ will result in judgment by Christ.

*To us now*: Luke provides us with an example of John the Baptist's preaching and summarises it in two ways. First, he proclaimed 'a baptism of repentance for the forgiveness of sins' (v. 3). Jesus the Saviour has broken into human history as promised. As God He brings God's long-promised salvation. The only appropriate response is one of far-reaching repentance. We must 'prepare the way for the Lord'. This is a repeated emphasis in both Luke and Acts. Without repentance there can be no forgiveness of sin, no membership of God's people, and no experience of God's blessings. No matter what a person's spiritual pedigree, previous experience, qualifications or privileges might be, repentance is a prerequisite to salvation. This repentance must be personal, genuine, and far-reaching. We must not invent or preach a gospel which sidesteps this truth. Nor should we allow the challenges of Jesus, designed to change our behaviour, to be watered down by appeals to the revised ethical standards of the world. Repentance, if genuine, will reach deep into relationships and habitual practices at home, at work and in the public sphere.

Second, the Baptist 'preached good news to the people'. John the Baptist's preaching *is* the good news of the gospel; the gospel preached by the Baptist is not separate from the gospel preached by Jesus. John's evangelism is Christ-exalting: 'he who is mightier than I is coming'. His evangelism offers the fresh start which his call to repentance demands. The Lord Jesus will flood His people with the long-promised Holy Spirit, thus enabling the work of repentance to take place. His evangelism warns of a coming judgment, with Jesus as the Judge, bringing salvation on the one hand, and on the other the 'unquenchable fire' of judgment. It is worth comparing John the Baptist's gospel proclamation with our own, and asking whether we are still proclaiming the authentic biblical gospel. We should expect opposition at the highest level as this message is proclaimed. But, with or without opposition, God will raise up children for Himself through the preaching of this Gospel.

## THE AIM

The aim of this study is to summon men and women to repent and receive the forgiveness of sins, and to show how this repentance and forgiveness are made possible in Christ.

## SUGGESTED INITIAL QUESTIONS

&#8227; Introduction
  &#8600; How did last week's study extend our understanding of both Jesus' mission and His identity?

&#8227; 3:1-14
  &#8600; How do verses 1 and 2 strengthen the historical credibility of Luke's writing?

  &#8600; Compare verses 2-3 with 1:76-79. What does this tell us about the heart of the gospel message?

  &#8600; Look up Isaiah 40:1-5. How does Isaiah's prophecy help us understand who the Baptist is, and who Jesus is?

- ↘ What does the Baptist consider to be lacking in the crowd?
- ↘ How does the statement at the end of verse 8, and the warning of verse 9, challenge what is lacking in the crowd?
- ↘ How do verses 10-14 help us make sense of what repentance really means?

✤ 3:15-30

- ↘ From verses 16 and 17, what does the Baptist tell us will be the key areas of Jesus' work?
- ↘ Look up Ezekiel 36:26-27. How is Jesus' ministry going to fulfil this promise?
- ↘ What is the difference between the Baptist's ministry and that of Jesus?

✤ Summary

- ↘ In verse 18, Luke summarises John the Baptist's ministry as, he 'preached good news' (i.e. he proclaimed the gospel). How does the gospel that *we* preach, or hear preached, compare and contrast with the gospel that the Baptist preached?

STUDY 6

# The Authentic Saviour
## Luke 3:21–4:13

## THE CONTEXT

Luke's narrative opened with the announcements of the impending births of John the Baptist and of Jesus (1:5-38). 'The Son of the Most High' was to be born to Mary. He would reign on the throne of His father David, and His kingdom, unlike David's, would have no end. Following the announcements, Mary, in her poem of praise, and Zechariah, in prophecy, explain the significance of these momentous events (1:46-80): God 'my Saviour' (1:47) had 'raised up a horn of Salvation' (1:69), and this Saviour would bring 'knowledge of salvation to his people in the forgiveness of their sins' (1:77). In chapter 2 the focus moves exclusively to Jesus. Once again, He is presented as a royal rescuer from God, 'a Saviour, who is Christ the Lord.' (2:11) The baby Jesus is greeted in the temple in terms of 'salvation' (2:30) and 'redemption' (2:38). The twelve-year-old Jesus presents Himself at the temple as God's Son whose essential work is His Father's work of salvation. John the Baptist and his ministry are described in 3:1-20; his message and his ministry are completely devoted to preparing people for the coming of salvation from God. The essence of his message is a command to repent, in anticipation of Christ's arrival as Saviour and Judge.

71

Throughout these introductory chapters, Luke has presented Jesus as the fulfilment of God's Old Testament promise to rescue His people. A key question still remains: is Jesus qualified for the task of salvation that Luke, and the Old Testament promises, have identified as His?

## THE STRUCTURE

3:21-22    Jesus is publicly identified as the Son of God – He is qualified as the Christ

3:23-38    Jesus is properly connected as the son of Adam – He is qualified as the Christ

4:1-13    Jesus is personally proven as the victor over Satan – He is qualified as the Christ

## OLD TESTAMENT NOTES

*The Son of God*: God's historic people, Israel, are described as God's Son in the Old Testament (Exod. 4:22; Hosea 11:1).

'*You are my beloved Son*': Psalm 2 identified God's anointed King specifically as 'the Son of God'. In response to the rebellious plots of the nations (v. 1), God laughs (v. 4), and announces the enthronement of His royal King (v. 6). This King is then declared to be His 'Son' (v. 7). God warns all kings and rulers of the earth to bow to His Son; those who 'take refuge in him' will be blessed (v. 12). This title, 'the Son of God', becomes a technical term by which God's King – the Christ – is known.

'*the Holy Spirit descended*': One of the marks of divinely anointed Old Testament leaders is that they are filled with the Holy Spirit (Judg. 3:10; 14:6; 1 Sam. 10:6 and 10; 11:6).

'*You are my beloved Son; with you I am well pleased.*': The rescue promised by God in Isaiah 40 (see Old Testament Notes for Study 5) is carried out by God's 'Servant'. Chapters 42 to 53 of Isaiah contain four 'servant songs' which spell out the identity and work of the servant figure. Isaiah 42:1 refers to him as 'my chosen, in whom my soul delights' (the word 'chosen' could also read 'beloved').

'*The son of Adam*': Adam and Eve, the first humans, rebelled in the Garden of Eden. Since that historic fall, all humanity has been tainted by Adam's sin, and is therefore under the judgment of God. God promised a rescuer who would come from the seed of Adam and Eve (Gen. 3:15), but though there had been many great heroes of the faith, no human had yet emerged who was free from sin, and therefore free from the judgment of God.

*'Man shall not live by bread alone.'*: Deuteronomy 8:2-3 explains God's purpose in taking His historic people, Israel, into the desert for forty years before they entered the Promised Land. The wilderness experience was designed 'to know what was in your heart, whether you would keep his commandments or not.' It was a test that God's people failed – repeatedly.

*'You shall love the Lord your God'*: Deuteronomy 6:4-5 provides a summary of the Law. God's historic people, Israel, had never kept it.

*'For he will command his angels concerning you'*: Psalm 91 is a Davidic Psalm in which God promised protection for His King.

## TEXT NOTES

### 3:21-22 JESUS IS PUBLICLY IDENTIFIED AS THE SON OF GOD

Luke has already drawn attention to the crowds of people who came out to be baptised by John (3:7, 10), and also to the expectation that John's ministry created among 'all' the people (3:15). Now in verse 21 he tells us that 'all the people' were baptised by him. In this context of public ministry and extreme heightened expectation, Jesus Himself is baptised. The baptism of Jesus demonstrates not His need for repentance and forgiveness, but His association with the people He has come to save. Jesus' baptism is accompanied by the visual, physical descent of God the Holy Spirit. The text does not say that the Holy Spirit descended as a dove, but that He descended in bodily form, like a dove. It was not a dove that descended, but something physical that looked like a dove. It is not the physical phenomenon, however, but the audible voice that explains what is happening.

A voice from heaven is a great rarity in the Bible – it is only on a very few occasions that God addresses His people directly. Here, in this very public setting, God speaks: 'You are my beloved Son;

with you I am well pleased.' (v. 22) His words would have reminded people of two great Old Testament passages, Psalm 2 and Isaiah chapters 42 to 53 (see Old Testament Notes), making it plain that Jesus is both His anointed King and His long-promised Servant. The significance of this incident in the life of Jesus, and also for understanding His ministry, cannot be overestimated. Jesus is being publicly identified as the Son of God the Father, and is being commissioned by Him. Years before the angel Gabriel had spoken to Zechariah, and to Mary, and the shepherds had been addressed by an angelic host, but now God speaks in person. Father, Son and Holy Spirit are all involved. Jesus is identified as the royal Ruler, before whom all kings and nations must bow in worship, and also as God's specifically chosen Servant, who will bring about the salvation of His people. This major event provides an initial answer to the question that arises from the first three chapters of Luke's Gospel: 'Is Jesus the authentic Saviour?' Yes, Jesus is qualified as God's royal Ruler. He has the personal commission of God. He is the Son of God.

3:23-38 JESUS IS PROPERLY CONNECTED AS THE SON OF ADAM

Genealogies in the Bible are designed to make theological points. The genealogy of Jesus is far more than simply a list of names. The reason for tracing His lineage is to demonstrate His royal succession from King David (v. 31), His descent from Abraham (v. 34), to whom God's promise of blessing was made (see 1:55), and His human identity as 'the son of Adam, the son of God.' (v. 38) Luke's aim is to show that Jesus is properly qualified, in every respect, as the Son of God.

Questions are raised by some about the differences between this genealogy and the one in Matthew's Gospel. The genealogy in Luke is in reverse order to the one in Matthew, and the first third of Luke's genealogy is almost entirely different to Matthew's. Also, Luke structures his genealogy differently, and there are various omissions and inclusions. These omissions and inclusions can be explained by the Jewish practice of Levirate marriage, which decreed that, when a woman's husband died, her husband's brother (or nearest

STUDY 6

male relative) was duty-bound to marry her and provide an heir. In an age when there was no state social care and when succession was vital for inheritance, this provided significant protection to the otherwise vulnerable. Levirate marriage meant, however, that lines of succession were often recorded as passing through a male relative, if the father of a child had died and the name of a later husband had been entered in a record.

This helps to explain the discrepancies, and may also be the reason why the first third of Luke's genealogy is so different. Matthew has Joseph's father as Jacob; Luke records Joseph's father as Heli. It may well be that one was the deceased husband of Joseph's mother and the other was the nearest male relative. The different structure, and the different order, is explained by the fact that Matthew and Luke had different purposes. Luke's aim is to show that Jesus is a son of Adam, the son of God. Jesus is fully human, and qualified, therefore, to be everything that Adam – and every other human since – had failed to be. He is not only 'the son of Adam, the son of God', He is also the long-awaited Christ, the Son of God.

4:1-13 JESUS IS PERSONALLY PROVEN AS THE SON OF GOD

The account of Jesus' baptism, and His genealogy, do not answer the question as to whether Jesus will be able to succeed where all others had failed. Adam was the son of God, Israel had been called 'God's son', and God's King David had been uniquely singled out as 'the Son of God', yet all had failed through temptation and sin. Now Satan questions Jesus' qualification: 'If you are the Son of God ...' (vv. 3 and 9). This passage has little to do with the personal temptation of twenty-first-century believers and everything to do with the testing and proving of Jesus. He is shown to be qualified as the one sinless, perfect human being who submits to God alone (v. 4), who worships God alone (v. 8), and who trusts in God alone (v. 12). Such a victor over Satan is qualified to save humanity. The forty-day fast in the wilderness is a deliberate mirror of Israel's forty years in the desert (see Old Testament Notes). This is a 'test' to see what was in Jesus' heart.

Full of the Holy Spirit and led by the Spirit (v. 1), Jesus is God's true anointed Ruler. The first test shows Jesus to be obedient to God's word – unlike Israel. The second test offers Jesus something that belongs to Him by right and that He will win afresh through His obedient death. So Satan's offer is, ultimately, empty, but it appears immediately attractive. Once again Jesus succeeds where Adam, Israel, David and others had failed. The third temptation is the most subtle of all. God had promised sufficient protection to His King (see Old Testament Notes), and Satan tempts Jesus to put God to the test by forcing the issue. Again, Jesus shows Himself to be perfectly qualified.

These three temptations pave the way for Jesus' ultimate victory over Satan at the cross, where Jesus' obedience, wholeheartedness, and trust will triumph. He is qualified as the Son of God.

## Key Themes

+ Jesus is perfectly qualified as the Son of God, God's Saviour of the nations: He is commissioned by God as His royal suffering Servant

+ He is connected by descent to David, Abraham and Adam

+ He conquers Satan

No other approaches Him in this regard. He is the Son of God, qualified to save humanity from sin.

## Application

*To them then*: In the first three chapters of his narrative, Luke has introduced Jesus as God's long-promised Saviour, who has come to rule eternally over King David's throne, and bring salvation to the nations through the forgiveness of sins. Luke has deliberately described the intense expectation that had built up around the birth of Jesus, and also His anticipated public ministry. Theophilus, Luke's reader, would rightly be hoping that Jesus would ultimately fulfil all the promises of rescue to be found in the Old Testament. The key question that remains, at the end of

Luke's introduction, is, 'Can Jesus meet the hopes that have been raised?' These verses provide a resounding 'Yes'. His commission as God's chosen King, anointed by God the Holy Spirit, also identifies Him as the Servant foreseen by Isaiah. Jesus is therefore confirmed as having come from God as God's rescuing Ruler. His links to David, Abraham and Adam qualify Him as a human saviour in fulfilment of God's heavenly promise. He is in a position to rescue humanity because He is one of us – the son of Adam. And He has the power to rescue humanity because He is God's King – the son of David, the Son of God. This leaves the final key question: 'Will Jesus stand the test of temptation or will He, like all others before him, yield to Satan?' He is tested in a setting that deliberately mirrors the context in which Israel, in the Old Testament, had so spectacularly failed. Where others had failed and fallen, Jesus stands. His credentials are flawless.

*To us now*: In a world where the results of human sin, the Fall, and God's judgment are in evidence everywhere, the need for a saviour is also everywhere apparent. Human 'solutions' are legion, but for every would-be saviour there is a corresponding disappointment. No other saviour has ever emerged as being genuinely qualified to deal with the root causes of all our problems – human sin and divine judgment. Unashamedly, Luke has identified Jesus as the unique Saviour. In this study we are shown that Jesus is qualified absolutely for the task.

## THE AIM

The aim of this study is to show that Jesus is uniquely qualified as Saviour to rescue humanity from sin and judgment.

## SUGGESTED INITIAL QUESTIONS

↳ Introduction

    ↳ What have we learnt so far in Luke about the identity and mission of Jesus?

    ↳ How does *who He is* qualify Him to do what He has come to do?

✤ 3:21-22

> ⅃ Read Exodus 4:22. How does God refer to Israel here?

> ⅃ Read Psalm 2. What does God tell us about His Son, the King, in verses 7-12?

> ⅃ Read Isaiah 42:1. What does God tell us about His servant?

> ⅃ In what ways do verses 21 and 22 of Luke 3 reflect Psalm 2 and Isaiah 42? Why is this significant?

✤ 3:23-38

> ⅃ Read verses 23, 31-32, 34 and 38. What is Luke seeking to show in his genealogy? Why is this important?

✤ 4:1-12

> ⅃ Read verses 3, 6 and 9. How do the temptations by Satan of Jesus relate to the study so far?

> ⅃ Read Deuteronomy 8:1-3. What was the purpose of Israel's time in the wilderness?

> ⅃ From verses 1-4, in what way does Jesus show Himself to be tried and tested where previously Israel and the leaders of Israel had failed?

> ⅃ From verses 5-8, in what way does Jesus show Himself to be tried and tested where previously Israel and her leaders had failed?

> ⅃ From verses 9-12, in what way does Jesus show Himself to be tried and tested where previously Israel and her leaders had failed?

✤ Summary

> ⅃ How has this study shown Jesus to be qualified for the task He has come to perform?

> ⅃ How does this give you confidence in the content and credibility of the gospel?

> ⅃ How does this strengthen our readiness to communicate the gospel?

# PART ONE (B)

LUKE 4:14 – 6:49

## *THE SAVIOUR'S MANIFESTO*

# Section Notes
## Part One (B): 4:14–6:49
## The Saviour's Manifesto

Luke's aim in writing is to give his reader certainty concerning 'the things which have been fulfilled among us'. He wants to give him confidence concerning the content and the credibility – historical, theological and socio-political – of the gospel, so that it will be communicated worldwide.

In the previous section, Luke has provided compelling evidence for Jesus' qualification as the long-awaited Saviour. He has embedded the account of Jesus of Nazareth in its immediate historical context, and also, importantly, within the expectation of Old Testament promise. This has provided clarification of Jesus' identity and His mission, for He has come as Saviour in fulfilment of what God had promised to Israel. His qualification has been confirmed not only by angelic, prophetic and divine word, but also by His genealogy and through His testing by Satan in the wilderness.

Chapter 4:14-15 indicates the beginning of Jesus' public teaching ministry in Galilee. Luke marks the start of a new section with the words: 'And Jesus returned in the power of the Spirit to Galilee … And he taught in their synagogues, being glorified by all.' Chapter 7:1 suggests the conclusion of this section as Jesus 'finished all his sayings in the hearing of the people'. The section opens with Jesus' 'manifesto' as He claims to be the fulfilment of the promise of Isaiah 61:1-2.

The manifesto of Jesus (4:18-19) has been the subject of significant debate. How readers understand the words 'the poor', 'the blind', 'the captives' and 'those who are oppressed' will have a significant impact on what they consider Jesus' mission to be. Luke has already indicated that he understands his account of Jesus' ministry to be an account of 'what has been accomplished', or fulfilled. He has rooted the interpretation of Jesus' identity and ministry in Old Testament promise. Thus, if Jesus' manifesto is to be interpreted with integrity, it must be understood in terms of what the prophet Isaiah meant by 'the poor', 'the captives', 'the blind' and 'the oppressed'. There are five key Hebrew words used by Isaiah for 'poor', variously translated as poor or afflicted or meek. With minimal exceptions, when Isaiah speaks of the poor and the afflicted he is referring to Israel, whose poverty and affliction have come as a result of her sinful rebellion against God.[1] In the final third of Isaiah, beginning at 40:1, God promises to His people, who have been oppressed in exile as a result of their sin, that He will provide 'double for all her sins' (40:1). One way of translating this verse reads 'a double'.[2] His afflicted (or poor) servant (Isaiah 53:4-6) will bear God's judgment on His people's sin. Thus God will deliver His people from the poverty, affliction, oppression and captivity that have come as a result of her rebellion against God, and God's consequent judgment. He will do this through a sin-bearing substitute who will save His people. This understanding of 'the poor' within the context of Isaiah is matched by a proper understanding of 'the blind'. In Isaiah, God's people are described from the outset as spiritually blind (Isa. 6:10). Indeed, God deliberately blinds them, in judgment (Isa. 29:10; 44:18) as a result of their sin. But, God promises that, through His Spirit-

---

1.  This understanding of the word 'poor' as referring to the 'humble', or indeed the meek or the afflicted, is confirmed by its use in the Psalms where King David is regularly described as 'poor' (Psalm 22:24; 34:6; 40:17; 70:5; 74:19). King David is the archetypal poor man.

2.  See footnote on page 52.

anointed warrior (61:1-2) and sin-bearing servant (42:6-7),[3] He will open the eyes of the blind.

Therefore Jesus' manifesto, viewed in its immediate and wider biblical context, has everything to do with His mission to rescue men and women from their own sin and spiritual ignorance, and from God's judgment, and little to do with economics, fair trade, environmental action or medical aid.[4] It has always been God's purpose to offer His rescue from sin and wrath to every human being, Gentile as well as Jew. Jesus warns the Jews in the synagogue that if they do not accept Him, He will go to the Gentiles, as Elijah and Elisha had done (vv. 26, 27). Hence His reference to the widow of Zarephath and Naaman.

If the 'manifesto' has been properly interpreted, it should be the case that Jesus' teaching in the synagogues of Galilee (4:20–6:49, i.e. the rest of the section) ties in with what has been proclaimed in 4:18-19. This turns out to be the case: Jesus makes proclamation of 'the good news of the kingdom of God' a priority over social action (4:42-44). He summons sinners into service (5:8-10), and declares sins forgiven (5:24). He has come to 'call … sinners to repentance.' (5:32) This agenda of providing salvation causes deep hostility among the religious (5:33–6:11), who are filled with fury. The religious elite of Jesus' day have long since given up on active belief in the God of the Bible. They show themselves to be not only

---

3. In Isaiah's prophecy God promises the rescue of His people through a figure who will be both a sin-bearing servant and a Spirit-anointed warrior. The image of the servant is developed in chapters 40–55; the image of the warrior is developed in chapters 55–66.

4. David Seccombe writes: 'There is nothing socio-economic or socio-religious about Luke's use of 'poor' terminology in the passages we have considered. To seek to ground liberation theology, or an ethic of poverty, upon these texts would be to misunderstand and misuse them.' Revd Dr David Seccombe, 'Possessions and the Poor in Luke–Acts', *Studien zum Neuen Testament in seiner Untwelt*, (Linz: 1982) Kenneth Bailey writes: 'Six hundred years of use (before and after Jesus) confirm the word 'poor' as meaning primarily those who tremble at the word of God (Isaiah 66:5).' Revd Dr Kenneth E. Bailey, *Jesus through Middle-Eastern Eyes* (London: SPCK 2008) p. 159.

hypocritical but also wicked in their opposition to the good salvation that Jesus has come to bring. Therefore Jesus, after a night of prayer, summons a new leadership for His people, and sets out how hearts will be changed, and lives will be transformed, among those who follow Him (6:12-49). This new people, with changed hearts, will carry the 'DNA' of their heavenly Father (6:35-36). Their renewed hearts will be transformed by the power of Jesus' words: He is the true guide who can see (6:39), and as Jesus' disciples build their lives on the 'rock' of His teaching (6:48), they will produce the good fruits of love, goodness, generosity and forgiveness (6:27-36).

## THE STRUCTURE OF PART ONE (B)

*4:14-44*    The Saviour's Manifesto

*5:1-32*    The Saviour's Mission

*5:33–6:11*    The Saviour's Offence

*6:12-36*    The Saviour's People

*6:36-49*    The Saviour's Pattern

# The Saviour's Manifesto
## Luke 4:14-44

## THE CONTEXT

Luke's aim in writing is to produce certainty in his reader concerning the things that have been accomplished. He wants to clarify for his reader the *content* of the gospel, to give him *confidence* as to the truth of the gospel, and to instil in him the *conviction* that the gospel must be declared to all nations. In the first part of his Gospel (1:1–4:13), Luke has introduced Jesus as a figure of history. Jesus is the Son of God – Christ the Lord – who has come as Saviour to bring God's long-promised salvation. This rescue is defined as 'peace' (1:79), by which is meant the peace with God that comes through the forgiveness of sins, as a person turns back to God in repentance. While Jesus' salvation will be available for 'all flesh' (3:6), it will be opposed vigorously. The reality of this opposition has been signalled by the imprisonment of John the Baptist for calling Herod to repentance. As for Jesus' credentials, these have been established by a direct word from God, by His genealogy, and by His unique defeat of Satan in the wilderness temptation.

With his introduction complete, Luke now turns to the teaching of Jesus (4:14–6:49). The section opens with a summary sentence, 'And he taught in their synagogues, being glorified by all.' The close of this section is signalled by the statement, 'After he had finished all his sayings in the hearing of the people' (7:1). The first scene in Jesus' ministry that Luke records is when Jesus delivers His famous 'manifesto' in the synagogue at Nazareth (4:18-19). This, together with its implications for Jesus' ministry, is then unpacked in the rest of the section. Numerous interpretations of Jesus' 'manifesto' have led to a variety of priorities for Christian ministry. However, the manifesto will only be understood rightly if its interpretation is matched by what follows in the rest of the section (4:20–6:49). Jesus has read from Isaiah, and in Isaiah the 'poor', the 'captives', the 'blind' and the 'oppressed' are people under the judgment of God. These are the people that Jesus has come to save, through the forgiveness of sins (5:24, 32). This is Jesus' priority in ministry, and Luke has arranged the second part of his Gospel in such a way as to help his reader to recognise this fact.

## The Structure

**4:14-19**    'He has anointed me to proclaim good news to the poor.'

**4:20-30**    The offence of Jesus' proclamation

**4:31-41**    The power of Jesus' proclamation

**4:42-44**    The priority of Jesus' proclamation

## Old Testament Notes

*'the poor', 'the captives', 'the blind' and 'the oppressed'*: In Luke 4:18-19 Jesus quotes directly (with minor alteration) from Isaiah 61:1-2. These verses form the heart of the central section in the final part of Isaiah's prophecy.[1] God's Spirit-anointed warrior,[2] whose conquering rule will bring salvation, speaks. His message is one of grace and judgment. Jesus' quotation from Isaiah 61 imports a sentence from

---

1.    David Jackman, *Preaching Isaiah*, (Ross-shire, Scotland: Christian Focus Publications 2010), pp. 243-4

2.    David Jackman writes: 'At the centre of this prophecy is Isaiah's portrait of a sovereign conqueror who will don the battle garments of God's anointed warrior and execute his righteous wrath in the just destruction of all God's enemies.' (59:14 - 63:6). Jackman, ibid., p. 243

Isaiah 58:6 ('to set at liberty those who are oppressed') and omits a reference to 'the broken hearted'. There is reference to 'the poor', 'the captives', 'the blind' and 'the oppressed'. Jesus' manifesto will be correctly understood only if the meaning of these words, in their original context in Isaiah, is understood. In Isaiah 'the poor' refers to God's historic people who have rejected God's loving rule, and are being afflicted by their enemies (the Babylonians) as a result of God's wrath and judgment. Isaiah uses five words, mainly, for 'the poor'. These refer almost always, and in particular in Isaiah 40 – 66, to the 'poverty' or 'affliction' that has come upon Israel due to God's judgment upon her. The 'poor' or 'afflicted' in Isaiah 40–66 will be saved through God's affliction falling upon 'the afflicted one' of Isaiah 53. Similarly, in Isaiah, 'the captives', 'the blind' and 'the oppressed' are God's people in captivity as a result of their rejection of God. God's people are blinded by God due to His judgment on their rebellion (see Isa. 6:8-13; Isa. 29:9-10) and are taken into captivity by the Babylonians as a result of their rejection of God. The 'year of the Lord's favour' is the year of Jubilee, a year when God gave rest to His people in the Promised Land.

*Elijah and Elisha:* The high point of the kingdom of Israel was under David and Solomon, but the kings who came after them rebelled against God's rule, and the kingdom was divided. King Ahab and his wicked wife Jezebel were amongst the worst rebels. Elijah and Elisha were the first great Old Testament prophets to call for repentance and the restoration of God's rule. Ahab ignored the summons to repent. Among those who did recognise Elijah and Elisha, and respond, were the non-Israelite widow of Zarephath (1 Kings 17:8-24), and Naaman, the commander of the army of the king of Syria (2 Kings 5:1-27).

*The kingdom of God:* Following the failure of David and Solomon, and their successors, God reiterated His promise to send a king and to establish His perfect kingdom (Isa. 9:6-7). God's perfect king would banish evil and re-establish God's people in God's perfect place to enjoy the blessings of God's presence. The duration of His reign was to be everlasting and the scope of His rule universal.

## TEXT NOTES

4:14-19 'HE HAS ANOINTED ME TO PROCLAIM GOOD NEWS TO THE POOR'

Verses 14-15 introduce this section which runs through to 6:49.
The subject matter is identified as Jesus' glorious teaching ministry.
In this section Luke has assembled material to show the reader the
substance of Jesus' message and ministry.

*vv16-19*: In quoting Isaiah 61:1-2, Jesus takes the pivotal verses
in the central part of the closing section of Isaiah's prophecy (see
Old Testament Notes). The verses could not be more significant,
nor Jesus' claim more substantial. Verses 18–19 consist of an
opening summary statement followed by four explanatory
clauses. There is proclamation in the summary statement, and
in the first and last clauses. Jesus signals that preaching and
teaching will form the essential core to His ministry. The phrase
'proclaim good news' (v. 18) translates the word 'to evangelise'
(see Text Notes for 3:18). The word is only ever used in the Bible
to speak of a verbal announcement. It is vital that this sentence
be understood in its original context in Isaiah; only then will
it be rightly understood on the lips of Jesus. Luke has already
encouraged his reader to understand Jesus' life and teaching in
terms of what was promised in the Old Testament, and what
Jesus is now accomplishing in fulfilling the Old Testament
promise. (1:1; cf. 24:45-47). The context of Isaiah 61 demands
that 'the poor' here is primarily a spiritual category referring to
those under God's just judgment. The 'blind', the 'captives' and
the 'oppressed' in Isaiah also refer to God's people experiencing
the wrath of God. His judgment had come as a result of their
sinful rebellion against Him. It took the form of spiritual
blindness, poverty and captivity, when the Babylonians defeated
them and deported them to Babylon (see Old Testament Notes).
Crucially, Jesus stops his quotation short, just at the point where
God announces His judgment and destruction on His enemies.

Isaiah 61:2 continues 'and the day of vengeance of our God', but Jesus does not include these words.

4:20-30 THE OFFENCE OF JESUS' PROCLAMATION

Jesus' announcement in verse 21, that 'Today this scripture has been fulfilled in your hearing', places His purpose in quoting Isaiah 61 beyond doubt. He is making a direct claim to be the Spirit-anointed warrior come from God to accomplish God's salvation of His people. Verse 22 causes significant difficulties for the translators. The first phrase could be translated as it reads in the ESV and the NIV, 'And all spoke well of him', or it could be translated as 'all spoke against him'. (It all hangs on whether the dative is one of advantage or disadvantage.) Given the subsequent attempt to murder Jesus (v. 29), it is perfectly possible that the synagogue congregation spoke against Him. They were taking offence, both at this local boy making such preposterous claims (v. 22), and at His cutting short the quotation from Isaiah, so as to exclude the prophecy of God's judgment upon His enemies. Jesus had quoted only the part of Isaiah 61:1-2 which speaks of God's grace. For a Jewish synagogue in enemy-occupied Galilee, this omission would be most unwelcome. They want Jesus to judge and overthrow their enemies. Jesus responds to the hostility of His family, friends and neighbours by quoting a proverb whose origin is unknown (verse 23). He then points His listeners to the work of Elijah and Elisha. While these great reforming prophets were rejected by God's people, they were recognised and welcomed by the most unlikely individuals from amongst the enemies of God's people, the widow of Zarephath and Naaman. Women and widows in ancient Israel were seen as an underprivileged and spiritually disadvantaged group, and Sidon was a Gentile city in Syria. Naaman was the Gentile commander of the army of Syria, one of Israel's most feared enemies.

By using these two examples from the history of God's people, Jesus makes explicit what was implicit in the truncating of the quotation from Isaiah: the time has not yet come for 'the day of vengeance of our God' (Isa. 61:2b). Instead, Jesus is introducing a 'window' of grace and favour for those who will respond rightly to the Lord's anointed (hence the phrase 'the gracious words that were coming from his mouth' in verse 22). By referring to the widow of Zarephath and Naaman, Jesus indicates that the identity of those who respond rightly to His ministry will be most unexpected. He really has come as a 'light for revelation to the Gentiles' (2:32). This further infuriates his listeners (vv. 28-30), and their attempt to murder the preacher at this early stage of His ministry confirms Simeon's prophecy (2:34). The people hate the idea that Jesus has come as Saviour to dispense grace to those who do not deserve it. Yet Jesus' authority, claimed in verses 16-21, is confirmed by His calm control in verse 30.

4:31-41 THE POWER OF JESUS' PROCLAMATION

The emphasis in these verses is on the authority of Jesus as He speaks; the power of His word is stressed in verses 32, 35, 36, 39 and 41. He has all God's authority to confront and drive back evil. In verses 31-32 the synagogue congregation at Capernaum is astonished at the authority of His teaching. This authority is then challenged by the man with the spirit of an unclean demon. The man identifies Jesus correctly as 'the Holy One of God' (v. 34) and recognises that Jesus' arrival signals the destruction of evil. The title 'Jesus of Nazareth' is deliberately specific – it identifies this Jesus, the Jesus who was Joseph's son, the Jesus of chapters 1 – 3. Jesus' commanding authority over evil amazes the congregation (v. 36) and the news of His power spreads (v. 37). In verses 38-39 the public display of His authority over evil is repeated in a private demonstration of authority over sickness. Simon's mother-in-law had a 'high fever' (v. 38). In the first century, without the benefits of modern medicine, her condition would have been a severe threat to her life and her recovery would have necessitated substantial convalescence. With just a word Jesus deals with the fever, and immediately she sets about her daily work.

Following these two demonstrations of Jesus' power and authority, it is no surprise that a great crowd of the sick and diseased gathered when the Sabbath was over (vv. 40-41). In verse 40 Luke stresses the absolute authority of Jesus: 'all those … any … every one of them'. Again, the demons identify Jesus accurately, and again Jesus has complete control over them. At this stage He appears eager to keep His identity hidden, and so He will not allow them to speak. Nonetheless, the three titles given to Jesus – 'the Holy One of God' (v. 34), 'the Son of God' and 'the Christ' (v. 41) – underline Jesus' claim in verse 21.

### 4:42–44 THE PRIORITY OF JESUS' PROCLAMATION

The people's desire for Jesus to stay in Capernaum (v. 42) is not surprising. His ministry had given them a glimpse of the heavenly kingdom promised by God in the Old Testament (see Old Testament Notes). He had emptied their hospitals, reduced the crime rate to zero, and rendered evil impotent. Jesus, however, has a bigger agenda than the short-term fix of one city's physical and social problems. Verse 43 is a key verse, recording how Jesus states the priority of His work: He has come to announce the arrival of God's kingdom. The phrase 'preach the good news' translates the word 'to evangelise' (see verse 18 and Text Notes on 3:18). Jesus resists the request to remain in Capernaum, sorting out immediate needs. His purpose is to herald the coming of the kingdom of God, and so He moves on to the synagogues of Judea.

## KEY THEMES

+ The identity of Jesus: Jesus is God's long-promised warrior King who has come to save God's people

+ The offence of Jesus' word: it is a day of salvation, offered even to His enemies

+ The power of Jesus' word: His word has absolute authority to save from evil and sickness

+ The priority of Jesus' word: the proclamation of God's Kingdom is His absolute priority

## APPLICATION

*To them then:* Luke's aim is to give Theophilus certainty concerning the things that have been accomplished. In recording Jesus' claim to be the fulfilment of God's promise in Isaiah 61, Luke clarifies precisely what it is that is being fulfilled by Jesus. The promise is for an end to the Israelites' exile, and rescue from the consequences of God's anger at their rebellion. Blindness, captivity, and oppression by God's enemies, in Isaiah, are all marks of God's judgment. So the poverty of God's people, though real, was a symptom of their spiritual rejection of God. Jesus had come to rescue God's people from the results of their sin.

In order to achieve his aim, Luke has to explain the hostility of so many to Jesus' ministry. Verses 20-30 begin to do this. Jesus' family and neighbours are unwilling to accept both the scale of His claim and the scope of His offer. These two themes run right through Luke / Acts: repeatedly, people will not accept that Jesus is God's rescuing King; nor will they accept that today is the day when God's offer of salvation is available to all types and conditions of men. Nonetheless, Jesus' power and authority over evil, and over all the consequences of human rebellion against God, are unrivalled. The evil powers declare Him to be the Son of God and the Holy One of God, and the authoritative power of His spoken words is acknowledged by all who hear Him. Luke wants Theophilus to grasp the authority of Jesus' word to accomplish everything He desires. Nothing and no-one can stand against Him. He is God's divine warrior King. When He speaks, God works. Above all else, Jesus' ministry is one of proclamation. His priority is to herald the coming of His Kingdom. Verses 15, 18, 19, 22, 32, 36 and 43 all stress the power of His word and the priority of preaching. Verse 43 and verses 18-19 together form Jesus' 'mission statement'. He came as a preacher to declare God's rescue – 'I was sent for this purpose.'

*To us now:* This opening passage in the public ministry of Jesus is designed to bring essential clarity to His mission. However, verses 18-19 are among the most widely misunderstood verses in the New Testament. It is vital, therefore, that we understand Jesus' quotation from Isaiah 61 in its original context, and that we do not 'import' our own understanding. Jesus' agenda has been set by the Old Testament promises of God; Luke does not want us to invent our own agenda for Him. The 'poor' in Isaiah are those who are under the judgment of God. The 'blind, captive and oppressed' in Isaiah are suffering as a result of their rebellion against their creator. Jesus has come as God's divinely anointed warrior King to announce God's rescue from the consequences of their sinful rebellion. His ministry does have social implications, but His ministry is not first and foremost to meet immediate social or physical needs. The priority of Jesus' ministry is stressed both in the 'manifesto' of verses 18-19 and in the mission statement of verse 43. He has come above all else to announce the coming Kingdom of God by speaking. Jesus sets this priority above all others, and He is even prepared to neglect the social and physical needs of Capernaum in order to focus on His work of verbal proclamation.

The priority that Jesus places on the spoken word should be held up as a plumb line by which to assess the value of all the ministries of a local church. Is our agenda the same as that of Jesus? Insofar as we diverge from His priority, to that degree we are sub-Christian. In announcing the availability of God's rescue, Jesus offends many, both by His claims about Himself and by His refusal to pronounce God's final judgment on His enemies. We need to be prepared for many to reject Jesus' offer of rescue because they will not recognise His right to rule – this is part and parcel of human rebellion against God. But even as many reject Him, we can expect to find the most unlikely people responding to Jesus. A window of time remains open, during which Jesus' offer of salvation from God's judgment is extended to all. While the work of proclamation may often appear weak, we can be sure that Jesus' words carry all His divine authority to achieve His work. It is by the proclamation of His authoritative word that evil is driven back and His work of rescue is accomplished. That this is a right reading of these verses will be confirmed in the following passages in this section (see 5:8, 24, 32).

## THE AIM

The aim of this study is that we should embrace the priority of Jesus' ministry, which is to proclaim the good news of His Kingdom to poor sinners facing the judgment of God.

## SUGGESTED INITIAL QUESTIONS

✤ Introduction

  ↘ List some of the ways in which Luke 1:1 – 4:13 has provided certainty for the reader concerning Jesus' identity and work.

✤ 4:14-19

  ↘ Read the first paragraph of the Old Testament Notes. Who are 'the poor', 'the captives', 'the blind' and 'the oppressed' in Isaiah's prophecy? From Luke 4:18-19, what does Jesus suggest He has come to do?

  ↘ How will He do it?

  ↘ What is the significance of Jesus' cutting short His quotation from Isaiah 61:1-2 at the place where He stops?

✤ 4:20-30

  ↘ What causes can you find in these verses for the anger of the synagogue congregation?

  ↘ Why are the widow of Zarephath and Naaman such good illustrations of what Jesus claims He has come to do?

✤ 4:31-41

  ↘ How do these verses help to confirm Jesus' claim in verse 21?

✤ 4:42-44

  ↘ What is surprising about what Jesus does not do in these verses?

  ↘ How do these verses, indicating Jesus' priority, confirm what He said in verses 18-19?

✤ Summary

  ↘ How does this study clarify Jesus' identity and mission?

  ↘ If we are to be faithful to His mission, what do we need to change?

STUDY 8

# The Saviour's Mission
## Luke 5:1-32

## THE CONTEXT

Dr Luke brackets this section of his Gospel with his comments on Jesus' teaching (4:15 and 7:1). The section as a whole concerns Jesus' teaching about His ministry. In the synagogue at Nazareth (4:18-19) He has spelt out His manifesto: He has come as the anointed warrior King, in fulfilment of Isaiah 61:1-2, to proclaim good news to the poor. The 'poor' are those who, on account of their sin, are under the judgment of God. Jesus' ministry of salvation will be pursued through His powerful word which liberates people from evil even as He speaks. The absolute priority of Jesus, ahead of even the most pressing physical and social needs, is to proclaim His coming Kingdom. This ministry of salvation from sin and God's judgment will result in the most unlikely individuals responding to Jesus and receiving God's blessing. Others will be offended by Him. Having laid out Jesus' manifesto, Luke now records Jesus acting it out. Jesus' ministry in chapter 5:1-32 is absolutely in line with the understanding of His manifesto as it was explained in 4:18-44.

## THE STRUCTURE

**5:1-11**     Jesus has authority to summon sinners to service
**5:12-16**     Jesus has authority to overthrow the effects of sin

5:17-26    Jesus has authority now to forgive sins
5:27-32    Jesus has authority to command repentance

## Old Testament Notes

Leprosy: Leprosy was a 'catch all' term given to a variety of skin diseases, some curable, others not. It was dreaded, and in its worst form it was disfiguring and, ultimately, deadly. When Moses and Aaron's sister Miriam was struck with it Aaron said, 'Let her not be as one dead, whose flesh is half eaten away' (Num. 12:12). Furthermore, only God had the ability fully to cleanse and heal the leper. When Naaman, the Syrian General, approached Israel's king for a cure, King Jehoram replied, 'Am I God, to kill and to make alive?' (2 Kings 5:7). The leper was spiritually excluded from the people of God because he was considered unclean. The Old Testament Law demanded that no defiled or decaying object should come before God's holy presence. God's people were to be set apart as an embodiment of all that was pure (Lev. 13:3, 46). The presence of disease was a mark of God's judgment on the Promised Land (Deut. 28:27; 1 Kings 8:37).

*The Son of Man:* Daniel 7:13-17 speaks of 'one like a son of man' being given 'dominion and glory and a kingdom, that all peoples, nations, and languages should serve him'. His dominion is described as 'an everlasting dominion' and His kingdom as 'one that shall not be destroyed.' This vision of the Son of Man, described at the heart of the book of Daniel, depicts Him as the absolute Lord and the final Judge of all peoples. He is the Davidic King par excellence.

## Text Notes

### 5:1-11 Jesus has authority to summon sinners to service

The section opens with Jesus following precisely the agenda that He had described as His priority in 4:42-44. The crowd is 'pressing in on him to hear the word of God' (v. 1) and He 'taught the people' (v. 3). The power of Jesus' word is emphasised in the next incident. Jesus' command to Peter, to let down his nets for a catch, appears futile, and Peter's exasperated comment in verse 5 is understandable. He and his companions had toiled all night and caught nothing; it was hardly likely that they would succeed in the midday sun. Peter, the professional fisherman, only agrees to Jesus the preacher-man's request because of the authority of Jesus' word: 'But at your *word* I will let down the nets.' The result is an astonishing haul (v. 6). Peter is immediately conscious of the supernatural nature of what has taken place, and also of the supreme power of Jesus and His word. He responds in the way that so many in the Bible do, when they are commissioned by God (Exod. 3:6; Exod. 19:16; Ezek. 1:28; Isa. 6:5). A genuine encounter with God always results, firstly, in an awareness of personal unworthiness and sin. Peter's 'Depart from me' (v. 8) is met by Jesus' 'Do not be afraid' (v. 10). This ties in with Jesus' statement of intent in His manifesto (4:18): He has come to proclaim good news to the poor, and Peter demonstrates himself to be one such. Peter's involvement in the miraculous catch is used by Jesus to show how He intends to employ sinners who turn to Him, as Peter has just done. Poor sinners are to be re-deployed by Jesus in the service of His kingdom. This service has, as its priority, precisely the priority of the King – 'catching men'.

Typically, Luke records the names of Peter's business colleagues, and this gives further historical credibility to his account. These three 'left everything and followed him'. Primarily, this incident is about Jesus' commissioning of three Apostles. On several occasions, in both his volumes, Luke is at pains to identify those who 'from the beginning were eyewitnesses and ministers of the word' (Luke 1:2; 6:12-16; 9:1-2; 24:48; Acts 1:21-23). The specific commissioning by Jesus of His 'eyewitnesses' and 'ministers' (or 'servants') further strengthens Luke's purpose – the building up of his reader's confidence. And it fits with this section of the gospel, whose theme is the authoritative word of Jesus. It is essential for Luke's reader that the sources, the individuals on whose testimony Luke has drawn, are genuinely commissioned by Jesus. At the same time, Peter's summons to service provides a model for every disciple. Jesus has stated the goal of His work, 'to proclaim good news to the poor'. When the poor sinner responds to Jesus, he or she is summoned to service. Not every disciple is called to leave everything in precisely the same way as Peter, James and John did. Every disciple must, however, place everything at Jesus' disposal.

## 5:12-16 Jesus has authority to overthrow the effects of sin

Jesus never draws absolute parallels between an individual's suffering and that individual's sin. Indeed, later in this Gospel, He refutes such clumsy connections (Luke 13:1-5). It is, however, the case that all suffering is connected in one way or another to the Fall (Gen. 3) and to God's judgment on this world. To that extent (while avoiding clumsy causal connections) suffering, sickness, disease and death in this world are a result of human sin. The Bible's treatment of leprosy underscores this point (see Old Testament Notes). Jesus' encounter with the leper is, therefore, an encounter with one who is suffering as a consequence of humanity's rebellion against God. This is a 'test case' to prove Jesus' claim in His manifesto (4:18-19). In verse 12 Luke, the doctor, provides a medical note on the man's condition: 'there came a man *full* of leprosy'. The man's request emphasises not only his faith, but also his helplessness (he is one of the 'poor', 'oppressed' and 'captive' of 4:18-19). Jesus' response emphasises both His compassion and His absolute authority to deal with the effects of sin. Jesus' touch of the man would have left the crowds gasping; normally it would have rendered Jesus unclean (see Old Testament Notes). The instantaneous healing confirms Jesus' authority as the Spirit-anointed warrior (see 4:20). The 'proof' of verse 14 – the word for 'proof' can also be translated as 'witness' – is intended to be evidence as much of Jesus' identity as it is of the man's healing. Jesus is wanting the synagogue authorities to be alerted to His arrival, and His divinity (see Old Testament Notes). This reading is confirmed by the assembly of religious bigwigs mentioned in verse 17. Once again, Jesus is reluctant to have news of His ministry spread widely beyond the disciples and the religious authorities. He has teaching work to do which will only be hindered by celebrity hunters.

## 5:17-26 Jesus has authority now to forgive sins

Of the Gospel writers who record this incident, only Luke spells out in such detail the make-up of the audience. Pharisees and teachers of the law assemble 'from every village of Galilee and Judea and from Jerusalem'. This is a serious theological examination of Jesus' ministry. Once again Jesus' authority is emphasised, 'the power of the Lord was with him to heal' (v. 17). Jesus' first words to the paralytic – 'Man, your sins are forgiven you.' – cause deep offence, but not for the reason most would expect. The theologians realise that Jesus is claiming authority to perform a work that is uniquely God's. All sin is ultimately against God. God alone is judge. Only God can forgive. If Jesus is not divine, then His rebuke 'Why do you question in your hearts?' (v. 22) displays an unparalleled arrogance. For the assembled theologians *both* healing the paralytic *and* forgiving his sins would be 'impossible' things (v. 23). Supernatural healing and divine pardon are in the hands of God alone. Verse 24 is key. The title Jesus takes for Himself is the title of God's divinely appointed royal Ruler and final Judge of all (see Old Testament Notes). Jesus wants the theologians to grasp that He does have authority here and now, 'on earth', to pronounce God's final verdict over an individual's life. This links directly to the 'job description' assigned to Jesus by Zechariah (1:67-79) and by the angels (2:11), and it is precisely in line with Jesus' manifesto (4:18-19). The miraculous healing authenticates for Jesus' audience His exalted claims. Once again the healing is instantaneous. There is no physio, no convalescence, no crutches. Jesus proves His authority to do one impossible thing by accomplishing another. The 'amazement' and 'awe' (v. 26) of the theological experts was as much at the physical healing as at Jesus' 'authority on earth to forgive sins'.

5:27-32 JESUS HAS AUTHORITY TO COMMAND REPENTANCE

The call of Levi is a logical 'next step' following Jesus' claim in verse 24. The first-century Jewish tax collector was neither friendless (Levi 'made him a great feast in his house, and there was a large company of tax collectors and others reclining at table', verse 29) nor impoverished. He was, however, spiritually beyond the pale. The occupying Roman forces contracted out tax collection to Jewish nationals. The tax collector had to gather revenue, but was allowed, by way of incentive, to add his own levy, taking his own cut. Tax collectors were, therefore, widely despised. Not only had they sided with the detested Roman forces, but also they usually became wealthy through extortion. Furthermore, their association with the pagan Romans made them spiritually unclean; they displayed total disregard for the affairs of both God and His people.

In His mission statement of verse 24, Jesus claimed to have come with authority, now, to pronounce the verdict of judgment day – He had 'authority *on earth* to forgive sins'. Levi is certainly 'a sinner'. Jesus summons him and he responds just as Peter, James and John had done. The grumbling of the Pharisees and scribes (v. 30) is no surprise when the company that Jesus keeps is considered (v. 29). Their dissatisfaction with Jesus' agenda shows their complete failure to understand Jesus' mission. Jesus' illustration (v. 31) and His explanation (v. 32) are not intended to teach that the Pharisees and scribes have no sin of their own. Rather, they reinforce the mission of Jesus as explained in His manifesto in 4:43 and in 5:24. He has come to summon sinners to repentance, and He has all God's authority to do so.

## KEY THEMES

- The work of Jesus on earth is focused on His offer of forgiveness of sins

- He has authority to pronounce God's final verdict of forgiveness over individual sinners

- He has authority to summon sinners and re-deploy them in His service

- He has authority to command and produce repentance in the most hardened sinner

- Ultimately He will overthrow all the effects of sin

## APPLICATION

*To them then:* The purpose of Jesus' coming has been spelt out in chapters 1 – 5 in terms of salvation. Zechariah was specific about the nature of the salvation that Jesus had come to bring: 'salvation … in the forgiveness of their sins.' (1:77) Jesus' manifesto (4:18-19), understood properly as a fulfilment of Isaiah's prophecy, is precisely in line with Zechariah's description of Jesus' mission. The salvation Jesus has come to bring was to be made available through the proclamation of His authoritative word. In 5:1-32 we find these themes being worked out and driven home in four progressive steps.

First, Peter's summons comes through the authoritative word of Jesus. Though he is a self-confessed 'sinful man' he is commissioned for service. This is not only an example of Jesus' work in saving sinners, but also, more importantly, it authenticates Luke's account (see below, *To us now*). Luke tells us that he has collected material from the 'eyewitnesses and ministers of the word' (1:2), people who were commissioned like the great prophets of old. Here we find Jesus appointing one of them – Peter. Next, Jesus heals a leper with a touch and a word. Luke's readers would have understood the implications of this far better than we. As King of God's Kingdom, Jesus has all God's authority to deliver on His claims. The immediacy of the leper's cleansing, the evidence given to the priests, and the rapid spread of the news all underline the authority of Jesus and His word. He is the Spirit-anointed warrior of Isaiah 61. Then, when Jesus heals a paralytic with just a word, His mission, now, 'on earth', is defined with pinpoint accuracy by His statement in verse 24. The fact that the healing of the paralytic was questioned by theologically literate people would have helped Luke's readers to understand precisely what Jesus' mission was: they questioned His authority to forgive sins, but He shows that He has God's authority. Thus He demonstrates that the salvation He had come to bring – the ultimate overthrow of the effects of sin – is possible because He, as the Son of Man, extends God's final verdict of forgiveness to individual men and women today, 'on earth'. This is the very heart of His work. It follows, lastly, that His agenda will be to summon sinners to repentance (cf. 1:77), as He does with Levi, but this is deeply offensive to the religious leaders who consider themselves to be 'well' and 'righteous'.

*To us now:* We can have confidence in Luke's account because it comes from those, like Peter, James and John, who were specifically commissioned by Jesus. His commission of them involved a recognition of their own sin and of their divine appointment. They were commissioned to serve others by calling them to follow Jesus.

We can have confidence in Jesus' power, ultimately, to overthrow all the effects of sin in this fallen world. He has authority to cleanse from sin and all the ravages of sin. His cleansing of the leper provides proof of His identity, and also gives us a snapshot of what He offers, ultimately, at the end of time, to every sinner who comes to Him.

We can have confidence in Jesus' authority here and now to forgive the sin of every man and woman who comes to Him in faith, as did the paralytic. Access to the salvation that Jesus promises is available because He has come with authority from God to pronounce sins forgiven.

We can have confidence, whoever we are, to turn away, like Levi, from whatever life we have lived and turn back to Jesus for forgiveness, because Jesus has come as a 'physician' for 'sick' sinners. This is the very essence of His mission and it defines the content of the gospel for us.

We should be confident that Jesus' agenda on earth is to bring salvation to His people through the offer of sins forgiven. This agenda of Jesus should be at the heart of every Christian disciple and every Christian Church. It will cause offence and grumbling among those who have failed to grasp that this is in fact Jesus' agenda, and who think that, on account of their own efforts, they have no need of a Saviour.

## THE AIM

The aim of this study is to clarify the mission of Jesus. He has come with all God's authority as Saviour, to declare sins forgiven.

## SUGGESTED INITIAL QUESTIONS

♘ Introduction

↘ What did we learn in the last study about the priority of Jesus in His mission?

✤ 5:1-11

  ↘ How does what Jesus is doing in verses 1-3 tie in with what He said His mission is in 4:42-43?

  ↘ What reason does Simon Peter give as to why he would (reluctantly) let down his nets?

  ↘ What causes Simon Peter's words and actions in verse 8?

  ↘ Why is Jesus' commission of Simon Peter so important for our confidence in Peter's ministry as one of Luke's 'eyewitnesses' (1:2)?

  ↘ In what ways does Simon Peter provide an illustration of Jesus' manifesto (4:18-19) and a model for all believers?

✤ 5:12-16

  ↘ Leprosy, while not an indication of an individual's personal sin, was a result of humanity's Fall (see Old Testament Notes). How do verses 12-16 illustrate Jesus' mission and authenticate His identity?

✤ 5:17-26

  ↘ Why are Jesus' words to the paralytic (verse 20) so shocking to the crowd of listeners?

  ↘ Saying *both* of the things suggested in verse 23 is impossible. What does Jesus demonstrate by healing the paralytic?

  ↘ How does this tie in with Jesus' priority as described in 4:18-19 and 4:43?

✤ 5:27-32

  ↘ Given what Jesus has said in 5:17-26, why is His summons of Levi the most obvious 'next step'?

  ↘ Try to put verses 31-32 in your own words. What does this tell us about Jesus' mission?

✤ Summary

  ↘ Summarise the mission of Jesus as explained in this study. How does that help to clarify what we learned in 4:14-44?

# The Saviour's Offence
## Luke 5:33–6:11

## THE CONTEXT

In Luke 4:18–5:22, Luke has recorded Jesus' manifesto for ministry, and also described some of the actions of Jesus that fulfil His manifesto. Jesus claimed to be the Spirit-anointed warrior, proclaiming 'good news to the poor'. The 'poor' have been identified as sinners under God's judgment. Jesus showed His authority to deliver on His promise by exalting the self-confessed sinner, Peter, into the service of the King (5:1-11); by overthrowing the devastating effects of sin (the leper: 5:12-16); by demonstrating His authority 'on earth' to forgive sins (the paralytic: 5:17-26), and by commanding repentance from a despised sinner (Lev. 5:27-32). The actions related in 5:1-32 confirm the interpretation of 4:18-19, that Jesus' priority is to proclaim to sinners the forgiveness of sins. But this does not meet with universal approval. The hostility first encountered in the synagogue at Nazareth is followed by a growing taking of offence among the religious leaders. The assembled experts consider Jesus' claims to be blasphemous (5:21), and the company He keeps to be inappropriate (5:30). They refuse to accept the implications of what they have seen and heard, both for the identity of Jesus and for the nature of His mission. In this section Luke records the rising opposition to Jesus and, at the same time, Jesus' exposure of His opponents' hypocrisy. This exposure of the Jewish establishment's true nature is necessary in order to strengthen His readers' confidence in the gospel.

## The Structure

| | |
|---|---|
| **5:33-39** | Jesus is the long-awaited bridegroom: it is time for change |
| **6:1-5** | Jesus is Lord of the Sabbath: the Law serves Jesus |
| **6:6-10** | Jesus fulfils the Sabbath: hypocrisy is exposed |
| **6:11** | Fury! |

## Old Testament Notes

*The Bridegroom:* In Genesis 2:24 Adam and Eve, created 'in the image of God', are brought together as husband and wife. This relationship is designed to mirror the true relationship with God for which all humanity is created. Thus God is presented as the husband of His people in Isaiah 54:5 and Hosea 2:7. God's King is depicted both in the Song of Songs and Psalm 45 as an ideal bridegroom to His people. God, as bridegroom to His people, promises His people that He has prepared a perfect wedding feast for them, where all that spoils this fallen world will be restored (Isa. 25:6-9; Amos 9:13).

*The Sabbath:* This was one day in seven set apart to mark out God's people as those who looked forward to the New Creation. Sabbath simply means 'rest'. In Genesis 2:1-3 God rested, or 'Sabbathed', on the seventh day. It is a mistake to think that God's seventh day rest was inactive. Genesis 2:2 says that God 'rested from all his work that he had done' – it does not say 'God finished work'. So God did not stop working, nor could God have been tired! Rather, God's 'rest', or 'Sabbath', was the purpose for which He created the universe. This Sabbath rest is then described in Genesis 2:5-25. It involves God and humanity living together in Eden, His perfect world. Following the Fall (Gen. 3) Adam and Eve were expelled from God's perfect rest and consigned to live in a world under God's judgment (Gen. 3:14-24). Under Moses, the Sabbath day was established in order that God's people might rest from physical labour. On the Sabbath they were to enjoy the relationship with God for which God had rescued them, and to look forward to the 'rest' of His New Creation which had been anticipated in the Garden (Gen. 2:1-3).

*King David and the Law:* Before David became King, but after he had been anointed, David was forced to flee from King Saul (1 Sam. 21:1-9). He took refuge at a place named Nob where the Tabernacle was. The High Priest Ahimelech had no food to give King David apart from the holy bread set apart in the Tabernacle. The Law forbade its consumption except by the priests of the Tabernacle (Lev. 24:9). Because David was in danger, Ahimelech allowed him to eat the bread of the Presence. Thus the Law was superseded on the grounds of the need of God's Anointed.

## TEXT NOTES

### 5:33-39 JESUS IS THE LONG-AWAITED BRIDEGROOM – IT IS TIME FOR CHANGE

The religious establishment's taking of offence at Jesus approaches crisis point as Jesus refuses to comply with their pious practice. The Law of Moses demanded that God's people should fast only once a year, on the Day of Atonement. The Pharisees, however, were particularly 'devout'. They fasted twice a week. This fasting was designed both to indicate humble mourning at sin and to intensify spiritual experience. Even John the Baptist's disciples prayed and fasted frequently. Jesus and His disciples did not fast, and verses 34-35 explain why. God, together with His anointed Messiah, are depicted as the ideal Bridegroom for His people (see Old Testament Notes). Jesus' question in verse 34, therefore, is far more than a call to 'be happy' – it is a claim at least to royalty, possibly divinity. Jesus' arrival as the Bridegroom for God's people means that fasting is as inappropriate to His disciples as it would be at any wedding. The Pharisees do not understand the times in which they are living (see 12:56). In Isaiah 25, the inauguration of the Messianic banquet necessitated celebration (25:9: 'This is the LORD; we have waited for him; let us be glad and rejoice in his salvation.').

However, while insisting that His arrival meant that it was time for celebration, Jesus would not allow His disciples to get ahead of themselves. Verse 35, in the context of intensified hostility, indicates that Jesus was already conscious of the cross, even at this early stage of His ministry. The phrase 'is taken away from them' suggests forcible removal.

The three parables of verses 36-39 confirm the extreme claim of Jesus in verses 34-35. The first parable (v. 36) speaks of the radically new nature of Jesus' work. Jesus cannot simply be 'tacked on to' the old. The second parable (v. 37) indicates the need for radical change in the structures of Israel's religion. The third parable (v. 39), which is unique to Luke, warns of the inevitable hostility to Jesus' radical new work. These verses lay out the implications of Jesus' manifesto for the established religious order of His day. He has come as God's anointed King, the Bridegroom of God's people. He has come with all God's authority, in the here and now, to declare sins forgiven (5:24). This has implications for the temple, the priesthood, the guardians of God's Law, and all the people. Now that the Anointed One has arrived the old ways are redundant. Jesus and His work cannot simply be tacked onto the old, nor can He be poured into the existing system of Israel's religion. Jesus is well aware that the religious leaders, who had grown so used to the Old Testament way of relating to God, were not going to like the implications of His manifesto (v. 39). They are more concerned for their own man-made additions to God's Law, and for their own religious reputation, gained by keeping up appearances. But it is time for change!

6:1-5 JESUS IS LORD OF THE SABBATH: HIS NEEDS SUPERSEDE THE LAW
In these verses Jesus drives home the teaching of 5:33-39 by showing how it applies to the Law and the Sabbath. The purpose of the Sabbath was for God's people to be marked out as those who were looking forward to His New Creation (see Old Testament Notes). As part of their extreme piety, the Pharisees had listed an additional 613 commandments to ensure that the Sabbath was kept. There were thirty-nine categories of forbidden work alone. Among these was the work of reaping. The Pharisees' accusation

(v. 2) is on the basis of their interpretation of the Law. Jesus' counter question immediately raises the stakes. He appeals to the precedent set by David in 1 Samuel (see Old Testament Notes).

This is a brilliantly chosen reference. Not only does it underline His claim to the Davidic throne, but also, because it is taken from a period in Israel's history when God's true King was being persecuted by a false pretender to the throne, it exposes the Pharisees' hostility. The situation in which Jesus and His disciples find themselves is remarkably similar to that of David in 1 Samuel. Jesus points out that when God's King was in need in the Old Testament, the requirement of the Law was superseded by the King's need for food. The Law, with its demands, was therefore to serve the King. The Pharisees should realise that a similar situation was confronting them now that Jesus, the true Bridegroom, was present. In case the implications of verses 3-4 were not clear enough, Jesus drives them home with extraordinary force in verse 5. Everything that the Sabbath anticipated is to be found in Him (see Old Testament Notes). The Sabbath was made for Jesus. He is the rest towards which the Sabbath looked. Now that He has arrived, all the Sabbath legislation is to be re-interpreted in the light of Him. God's King supersedes the Law and the Law serves God's King. New wine requires new wineskins!

### 6:6-10 JESUS FULFILS THE SABBATH: HYPOCRISY IS EXPOSED

This second Sabbath incident results in the religious establishment's hostility rising to a murderous pitch. The theological elite are now seeking confrontation; they want 'a reason to accuse him' (v. 7). Just as with the establishment inspectorate (5:22), Jesus 'knew their thoughts' (v. 8). His deliberate decision is designed simultaneously to confront and to expose hypocrisy. The question in verse 9, together with the intense examination in verse 10 and the subsequent miracle, provide the most compelling evidence so far that the old garment and old wineskins of the religious establishment need replacing. On the Sabbath the people of God were meant to be looking forward to a New Creation where the Lord restored all that is broken in this fallen world (see Old

Testament Notes). Jesus has self-evidently come as Bridegroom (5:34) and Son of Man (6:5) to save. The Pharisees are so intent upon protecting their man-made rules that they are neither willing to 'do good' nor to 'save life' on the Sabbath. Such is the hypocrisy of man as he rejects his maker that he chooses 'harm' over 'good' and 'destruction' over 'salvation'.

6:11 FURY!

The phrase 'what they might *do* to Jesus' is ominous. It anticipates the murderous fury which ended ultimately at the cross.

## KEY THEMES

| | | |
|---|---|---|
| ✦ | The identity of Jesus: | Jesus is the long-awaited Bridegroom – God's King |
| | | As King, Jesus is the lord of the Sabbath |
| | | Jesus, Lord of the Sabbath, has come to accomplish the 'good' and the 'salvation' which the Sabbath anticipates |
| ✦ | Fulfilment and change: | Everything that the Sabbath and Old Testament Law anticipate is fulfilled in Jesus. It is time for radical change |
| ✦ | Exposure: | Rejection of Jesus and His salvation will be exposed as hypocrisy |

## APPLICATION

*To them then:* A major part of Luke's aim in this Gospel is 'that you may have certainty concerning the things you have been taught' (1:4). So far in the Gospel Luke has strengthened his readers' confidence by underscoring the historical and theological integrity of Jesus' work. In this passage he begins to address the religious establishment's hostility towards Jesus. This theme will be developed significantly in the rest of the Gospel. Verse 39 of chapter 5, a verse unique to Luke's account, indicates that this is his aim here. He wants his readers to understand *why* Jesus' opponents are so hostile towards Him, and to see that their hostility says far more about their hypocrisy than Jesus' credibility. The rejection of Jesus by the Jewish religious establishment would have been a significant stumbling block to belief in the first century. Why do the Jewish leaders, of all people, not believe? Jesus' argument is on the basis of His identity – He is their long-awaited Bridegroom and the Lord of the Sabbath. It is time for change! Nothing can ever be the same again for the Jews, now that Jesus has arrived. His work, fulfilling all the Old Testament promises, requires new structures.

Jesus recognises that the leaders of the old order will not like this. But there is precedent even in the Old Testament for the Law to serve God's King (6:1-5). Jesus has come in fulfilment of the Sabbath as King and Saviour 'to do good' and 'to save' (v. 9) – just as the Sabbath anticipated. Religious hostility of any sort, even in the name of the Law, shows hostility to God and to the saving good that God wants to do. It is, thus, pure hypocrisy to reject Jesus on the grounds of religious order, and the establishment's rejection shows them for what they are. Their furious and murderous response should be seen for what it is. Jesus has all God's authority to do the good of saving men and women for His New Creation. Hatred of Jesus is hatred of God.

*To us now:* Rejection of Jesus by ruling establishment powers is as unsettling today as it was in the first century – all the more so when the powers concerned claim religious pedigree or moral high ground. Whether it is the 'established' denominations (Church of England, Roman Catholic), or another religion (Islam, Hinduism), or simply the secularist politically correct, the governing authority's rejection of Christ can result in real uncertainty for the believer. By including this material, Luke shows this rejection for what it is. Jesus' identity as King and Saviour qualifies Him uniquely for the work He alone can do – the Sabbath work of salvation and, ultimately, of New Creation. To oppose Jesus is to oppose what is good. To choose man-made religious structures (however beneficial they may appear) in opposition to Christ is to stand against what is good and what saves life. It is to choose harm over good; destruction over salvation. Believers should anticipate a furious reaction when this is pointed out.

Applications of this point are legion. For example, refusing to allow someone to speak of Jesus in their workplace, on the grounds of diversity, will rob people of the very truth that has power to liberate them from sin and guilt; or, preventing teachers from making Jesus known appropriately, in a school, will deny children the very truth that would see their lives established on solid foundations. Wherever anyone or anything opposes the work of Jesus, this person or body is working against the good of humanity. This is true wherever it takes place and by whatever means. Legislative bodies, political hierarchies, workplace communities, educational establishments, other religions and even mainline denominations can be working for harm rather than good if they oppose the work of Christ. Christians need to see this clearly or they will be far less courageous in presenting the gospel when faced with hostile rejection.

## The Aim

The aim of this study is to see that all opposition to Jesus, on whatever grounds, is hypocritical rejection of what is good.

## Suggested Initial Questions

- ✤ Introduction
  - ↘ How did Jesus' statement in 5:31-32 summarise what He had taught in 5:1-30?
- ✤ 5:33-39
  - ↘ Who is Jesus claiming to be in verses 33-35 (see Old Testament Notes)? Why would fasting have been so inappropriate for His disciples?
  - ↘ What different aspects of Jesus' new work are identified by each of the three parables in verses 36-39?

✤ 6:1-5

  ↘ What was the Sabbath rest intended for (see Old Testament Notes)? So what was Jesus claiming when He spoke the words in verse 5?

  ↘ Why is Jesus' comparison of Himself with King David so telling?

✤ 6:6-10

  ↘ By opposing the good Sabbath work of Jesus, what do the Pharisees show about themselves? In which modern-day philosophies and religious structures do we find this same hypocrisy?

✤ 6:11

  ↘ What does this statement tell us about the opposition to Jesus?

✤ Summary

  ↘ What have we learned in this study about the opponents of Jesus? What is it that they hate about Jesus? Where do we see this hypocritical Pharisaism today? How does Jesus respond?

STUDY 10

# The Saviour's People
## Luke 6:12-36

## THE CONTEXT

Luke 4:14 – 6:49 is a record of what Jesus 'taught in their synagogues' in Galilee (4:14-15). Luke has recorded both Jesus' manifesto (4:18-19) and His subsequent actions which are in line with His manifesto. Jesus has come 'to proclaim good news to the poor'. This proclamation involves summoning sinners into service (5:1-11), delivering a leper from the consequences – in his case dreadful and extreme – of living in a sinful, fallen world, and healing a paralytic, forgiving him his sins at the same time. Jesus is the Son of Man and, as He takes the role of the end-time judge, He declares, in the present, His verdict of judgment day (5:24). His summons is available to even the most hardened sinner (5:27), for He has come to 'call ... sinners to repentance'. This radical agenda of Jesus rocks the religious leaders, who complain (5:29-32). In response, Jesus drives home His teaching. He stresses the radical new nature of His work and He exposes the hypocrisy of the religious establishment. Attempts by the religious to create their own righteousness achieve precisely the reverse. The whole system of man-made philosophy and religion does harm, not good – it ruins and destroys life (6:9-10). The establishment react to Jesus' diagnosis not in repentance, but in fury (6:11).

It is in this context that Jesus now summons and appoints His twelve Apostles – a new leadership for the people of God. In verses 12-19 Jesus establishes the foundation of His new people (the 'building blocks' of the Apostles). He goes on in verses 20-36 to describe what it looks like to become part of His family, and then how to live as a member of that family.

## THE STRUCTURE

| | |
|---|---|
| **6:12-19** | His people's foundations |
| **6:20-26** | Family profile |
| **6:27-36** | Family likeness |

## OLD TESTAMENT NOTES

*The twelve tribes of Israel:* The twelve sons of Jacob were the fathers of the twelve tribes of Israel. They were foundational figures. The Old Testament people of God traced their genetic origins to them. At Mount Sinai, Moses chose leaders from the twelve tribes as heads over them (Deut. 1:9-18). The symbolic significance of the twelve tribes as representing all the people of God is confirmed in John's vision of the City of God (Rev. 21:14).

## TEXT NOTES

### 6:12-19 HIS PEOPLE'S FOUNDATIONS

*vv12-16:* In its context, Jesus' appointment of twelve Apostles is both highly significant and profoundly provocative. He has just exposed the absolute failure of Israel's leadership and the need for new 'wineskins'. Now He appoints twelve new leaders.

*The divine commission:* His night of prayer on the mountain emphasises the divine commission of the Twelve. This commission mirrors Moses' appointment of leaders for God's people at Mount Sinai (see Old Testament Notes). The language emphasises His deliberate choice of the twelve for this foundational role (v. 13). This language of choice is repeated at the appointment, later on, of both Matthias and Paul (Acts 1:24; 9:15).

*The unique task:* The word 'Apostle' means a person 'sent forth'. It is used of someone to whom a particular responsibility is given. The qualifications required of an Apostle were not only to have been 'chosen' but also to have been witnesses of the life of Jesus and His resurrection (1:2-4; 24:45-49; Acts 1:21-22).

*The specific group:* The divine commission and the unique task were reserved for those who are named; their identities are carefully recorded and preserved. At first sight it seems that there is a discrepancy between the records of names in Matthew, Mark and Luke. Luke records two Apostles with the name Judas (v. 16), Matthew and Mark have no second Judas but include Thaddaeus. Dr Richard Bauckham has demonstrated that it was normal in first-century Palestine for people to have two names and to be referred to by either.[1] Given the actions of his namesake, the choice of Judas the son of James to be known by his alternative name 'Thaddaeus' is not hard to understand. Luke's careful recording of the names, the commission, and the task of the Apostles is designed to give confidence to his reader (see Application below).

*vv17-19:* The vast crowd of disciples and the great multitude of people, from within the borders of Israel and beyond, experience at first-hand the power of the Lord of the Sabbath. The universal healing ('all the crowd… healed them all') demonstrates both His identity as God's King and His mission to save, ultimately, from the ravages of sin. The teaching that follows, known as 'The Sermon on the Plain' (verse 17), extends to the end of the chapter.

### 6:20-26 FAMILY PROFILE

*The focus of God's favour:* To be blessed by God in the Bible is to be the focus of His favour. Great care needs to be taken in verses 20-26. The words "poor", 'rich', 'hungry' and 'full' must be read according to their context in Luke's Gospel. Jesus has already used the term 'poor' and placed it firmly within the context of Isaiah's prophecy (see Old Testament Notes in Study 7). The 'poor', 'the captives' and the 'oppressed' in Luke 4:18 do not refer to all who are materially disadvantaged anywhere, but to those who recognise their spiritual poverty, the result of sin and God's judgment. The context, for

---

1.   Bauckham, ibid., pp. 93-112

verses 20-26, is again the key to correct understanding. Verses 20-22 are bracketed by the phrases 'he lifted up his eyes on his disciples' and 'on account of the Son of Man'. Thus, in verses 20-24 the 'you who are poor', the 'you who are hungry', the 'you who weep now', and the hated, excluded, reviled and spurned – these descriptions all refer specifically to Jesus' disciples, who come to face the same kind of rejection that He Himself has already experienced (4:29; 5:30; 6:11). Once again, Jesus is not making a universal promise to all materially poor people everywhere. Nor does God's favour rest on all sad, hungry, or dispossessed people. This promise of God's favour is for those who recognise their spiritual poverty and follow Jesus; in following Jesus they will experience rejection and exclusion, with their master.

The 'woes' of verses 24-26 must also be read carefully in the light of their context. Verse 26 is a key indicator to who Jesus is speaking about. The Jewish establishment is in the process of rejecting Jesus (6:11). They are the 'false prophets' of Jesus' day. They may well be popular (verse 26), wealthy (verse 24), well-fed and happy (verse 25), but if they reject Jesus they are just like the false prophets of old. Thus Jesus' 'woes' are not universal statements condemning all who have money, food, happiness and friends. This is a condemnation of the unbelieving establishment figures who reject God's true King (the Bridegroom and Lord of the Sabbath), preferring all that the world has to offer.

*The experience of God's favour*: The contrast between present and future experience runs right through verses 20-26. The juxtaposition of 'now' and 'for you shall be ...' is found in verse 21 (twice) and verse 25 (twice). Verses 22-23 contrast present experience with future blessing. Verse 24 makes clear that those who make present wealth a priority over self-denying discipleship have received all they are going to get from God. The present experience of a true disciple will mirror the past experience of genuine prophets (verse 23). True disciples, like the prophets of old, should expect to experience real material disadvantage. There will be great contrasts between the Christ-rejecting world and the genuine disciple. Present experience, however, is no reliable barometer for future blessing. Appearances can be deceptive. God's favour is reserved for those who follow the Son of Man (v. 22). His condemnation rests on those who reject Him (v. 26). This section is essential if Luke's reader is to remain confident as a genuine disciple of Christ.

### 6:27-36 FAMILY LIKENESS

The command to 'love your enemies' comes twice in this section, like a pair of brackets (vv. 27 and 35). Verses 35-36 provide a succinct summary of the key principle. The issue is one of family likeness. Jesus' point is not that loving enemies *makes* a person a child of God, but rather, that love, goodness, and generosity are all characteristics of God. He shows kindness to those who are not only ungrateful but also evil. Mercy is the nature of God.

*vv27-31 The family DNA:* In verses 27-28, Jesus instructs His disciples on how to respond to the hostility of the world. The context is important: 'enemies', those who hate, abuse and curse the disciples of Jesus, are enemies of the gospel and of gospel people. These verses must be read in light of 6:11. In verses 29-30 Jesus explains what it looks like in practice to 'love your enemies'. His commands are profoundly counter-cultural. To be struck on the cheek is to face public humiliation, so to turn the other cheek would mean acceptance of that humiliation. The cloak was the equivalent of a coat or a jacket, the tunic was the shirt, so not withholding the tunic would mean giving away virtually all one's clothing. The word 'give' in verse 30 is in the present continuous tense – give and go on giving. To have goods taken away is to be stripped unjustly of possession. Jesus encourages weakness in the face of hostility, vulnerability in the face of opposition, generosity in the face of need, and a readiness to sit loose to possessions. The Christian disciple will frequently experience intense opposition. The hatred of the world will be directed towards Jesus' followers, but the response modelled by Jesus is to be mirrored by His people. As children of a merciful Father, they are to show a true family likeness. This standard of family life is encapsulated by the so-called 'Golden Rule' in verse 31, teaching that is unique to Jesus. It suggests deliberate action focused entirely on the absolute good of the other, to the disadvantage of self.

*vv32-36 The family demands:* Jesus' explanation of His family's DNA calls for some qualification. He offers none! His repeated comparison with those who are not His people – 'even sinners' (vv. 32, 33 and 34) – emphasises the logic of His teaching even as it drives home the challenge. The Father does not work with mercenary incentive; nor should His children. The essence of the Father's character is generosity, goodness, and love. His love is shown to the ungrateful and the evil. He shows mercy simply because He is merciful. Membership of His family demands an exhibition of the Father's character. Failure to grasp this is a failure to grasp the seriousness of the call to discipleship.

## KEY THEMES

+ Confidence in the Apostles' teaching as the foundation for God's family

+ Clarity on the experience of discipleship –then, and now

+ Challenge to live as disciples

## APPLICATION

*To them then:* The careful recording of the appointment and naming of the twelve Apostles has a purpose; it is designed to give real confidence as to the identity of the 'eyewitnesses' on whom Luke's account depends. That these twelve were known by name, and were deliberately appointed with divine authorisation for the specific task of Apostleship, is important for confidence in their testimony. Professor Richard Bauckham describes them as 'an authoritative collegium' which existed in Jerusalem for some years at the beginning of the church's history (see Acts 1–5)[2]. If any group in the early church was responsible for the transmission of Jesus' teaching it was this group. They are the 'fresh wineskins' (5:38) – the new leadership – of the people of God. Jesus' deliberate appointment of twelve new leaders

---

2.  Bauckham, ibid., p. 94

for the people of God, at precisely the moment when members of the establishment show their determination to reject Him, is highly significant. It indicates for Luke's reader that Jesus' saving work will involve establishing a whole new foundation for God's people.

By carefully describing the present and future experience of His people, Jesus guards new disciples against false expectations. This also strengthens confidence. Careful reading of the passage (vv. 20-26) eliminates any possibility that Jesus might be making general or universal promises to all poor people, or all the materially or socially excluded. Verses 20-23 are targeted directly at Jesus' disciples, and verses 24-26 at those who reject Jesus in order to cling to present popularity and reputation. Just as Jesus was hated, excluded, reviled and rejected, so too will His disciples be in the present. Right expectations of God's favour will guard Jesus' disciples against dashed hopes. Because hostility for following Jesus is a mark of discipleship, so His persecuted people can afford to leap for joy, even as they experience hostility. They are favoured by God.

The challenge of verses 27-36 is aimed particularly towards the response, by Jesus' disciples, to those who persecute them. Even in the first months of the church's life, persecution against believers broke out (Acts 8:1-4). Believers lost everything. Jesus challenges His followers to respond to this kind of hostility as children of their heavenly Father by showing mercy.

*To us now:* We should have no doubt that Jesus' saving work is a radical fulfilment of all that the Old Testament promised. His commission of the twelve Apostles suggests a completely new foundation for the people of God. The place of these twelve, and the particularity of their authoritative eyewitness testimony as the foundation for the church, is confirmed by the rest of the New Testament (e.g. Eph. 2:20; Rev. 21:14).

The first disciples regularly faced hostility from the world. Verses 20-26 would have reassured Luke's original readers that their experience was valid. Every generation of true believers discovers the reality of these verses. Hostility to Jesus and His family, from legislators, media, colleagues and close family members, is nothing new. These verses should give great encouragement. We may be 'poor' compared to those who reject Jesus, and we may experience sadness, both at the sin of the world and at our own sin; some may even find themselves deprived of the basic necessities of life. But God's favour rests on His persecuted church, as Christians follow Jesus and name His name. Those who suggest that earthly wealth, health, popularity, promotion, pleasure and possessions are the expected norm for Christian disciples are neither teaching nor following the Jesus of the New Testament.

The challenge of verses 27-36 speaks for itself. The way we respond to those who persecute us is to be modelled on the character of our Father in Heaven. We are to be marked out as entirely different from 'sinners'. The applications of these verses are legion. Biblical churches increasingly face rejection, both from the world and from traditional denominations and their officials. Individual Christians will regularly face discrimination. We must respond in love, kindness, mercy, blessing and prayer.

## THE AIM

The aim of this study is to understand true discipleship and so to stand firm and confident as a disciple.

## SUGGESTED INITIAL QUESTIONS

  ↻ Introduction

  ↘ What produced the furious reaction in 6:11?

  ↻ 6:12-19

  ↘ In the account of Jesus appointing the Twelve, there are several features designed to give the reader confidence in the 'eyewitnesses', whom Luke has interviewed in order to write his Gospel. What are these features?

  ↘ How do verses 17-19 increase our confidence in the work of Jesus?

  ↻ 6:20-26

  ↘ Who is Jesus speaking to in these verses? What is the cause of their poverty, hunger, sadness and exclusion? (See 6:11 and 22.)

↘ What should disciples of today expect from following Jesus? Why should this make us happy?

↘ How do verses 24-26 relate to both 6:11 and 6:22?

↘ Who, then, are the 'rich', the 'full', the 'happy' and the popular in these verses?

✢ 6:27-36

↘ Verse 36 governs these verses. What does Jesus expect of His followers?

↘ How do verses 27-31 illustrate the Father's mercy? What would it look like, practically, for us to live like this at home and at work?

↘ What action does Jesus expect of His followers in verses 32-35? What will it look like practically for us to live like this at home and at work?

↘ What will this required action (vv. 32-35) indicate to others?

✢ Summary

↘ This section began with Jesus' manifesto to proclaim good news to rescue poor sinners (4:18-19). What do these verses (6:12-36) tell us about what Jesus is summoning forgiven sinners to be?

STUDY 11

# The Saviour's Pattern
# Luke 6:36-49

## THE CONTEXT

Chapter 7:1 indicates the start of a new section of Luke's 'orderly account'. So this passage, 6:36-49, brings to a conclusion the teaching of Jesus which began at 4:14-15. His teaching can be divided into four parts.

| | |
|---|---|
| *4:14-44* | Jesus has come with the priority of proclaiming the good news of the Kingdom. |
| *5:1-32* | He has come to summon sinners into His Kingdom. |
| *5:33–6:11* | His Kingdom needs fresh structures – and the leaders of old order will detest this. |
| *6:12-49* | The people of His Kingdom are His disciples. These disciples are: a people led by the twelve Apostles through their teaching (6:12-16); the true people of God who are 'blessed' even as they are reviled 'on account of the Son of Man' (6:20-26), and a radically counter-cultural people whose 'DNA' is that of the Father (6:27-36). |

Throughout the closing verses of this section, Jesus has had one eye on the current leadership of Israel. He has all but named them as false prophets (6:26). In verses 27-36 He gave instruction on how His disciples were to respond to their enmity. The section now concludes with a final warning about their teaching and an assurance about the true people of God.

## THE STRUCTURE

**6:36-45**    Choose your teachers with an eye on their fruit
**6:46-49**    Build your house with an eye on the future

## OLD TESTAMENT NOTES

The Flood: From the days of Noah (Gen. 6–9), the image of floodwater has been used in the Bible as a picture of both personal calamity and, ultimately, God's final judgment. Psalms 42:7 and 144:7 are examples of the former; Isaiah 30:28, Nahum 1:7-8 and 2 Peter 3:6-7 of the latter.

## TEXT NOTES

### 6:37- 45 CHOOSE YOUR TEACHERS WITH AN EYE ON THEIR FRUIT

*vv37-38:* These verses continue Jesus' instruction in verses 27-36. As 'sons of the Most High' (v. 35) and children of a merciful Father (v. 36), Jesus' disciples are to be radically counter-cultural. The command to 'judge not' (v. 37) is not an instruction against discernment – Jesus is about to warn His disciples that they need to be discerning about 'blind' teachers. Rather, Jesus is speaking against judgmental, condemning, unforgiving hearts. This general statement has particular reference to His disciples' attitude to their persecutors (v. 22-23). As with the instruction in verses 27-35, these attitudes are the outworking of the family DNA; behaviour that is in line with the family character will be richly rewarded (v. 38). To understand the picture in verse 38, we need to know that the first-century garment was a long, flowing robe with significant amounts of surplus cloth. This material (from 'the lap') could be pulled up above the belt and used as a receptacle for carrying grain from the market. Jesus is promising abundance for those who treat their persecutors in a Christ-like way. The emphasis on the future in verses 21-23, together with the expectation, in these verses, of suffering, suggests that the timescale in verse 38 is not necessarily the present.

*vv39-40:* The parable in these verses confirms what has been the background to Jesus' teaching in verses 37-38. He has been speaking against the Pharisees and teachers of the law, even as He has been instructing His disciples. Jesus is warning His followers, the true people of God, against the judgmental hypocrisy of the religious establishment (6:6-11). If His disciples continue to follow the Pharisees, they will end up like them. When the blind lead the blind there is only one outcome – falling into a pit.

*vv41-45:* The connecting word 'for' (vv. 43, 44 - twice) indicates that verses 41-45 are tightly tied together as one unit. The question in verse 41 connects this verse to verses 39-40. It suggests that those who listen to blind guides and false teachers are as much the target audience of these words as the false teachers themselves. Jesus is seeking to wean His disciples away from the phoney religious leaders, helping them to recognise the fruit they produce, while at the same time teaching them what it looks like to be a true child of the Father and a son of the Most High. The 'speck' (v. 41) is a speck of sawdust or dirt. The 'log' was the main beam, the structural support running across the centre of a house and holding the roof and walls together. The image is meant to appear absurd. Jesus wants the members of His Kingdom, the true people of God, to be free from hypocrisy.

The image of the tree and its fruit (vv. 43-44) is self-explanatory, but the context (vv. 40-42) suggests that it is the false teachers that are in view. The teaching of the Pharisees produces only the bad fruit of hypocritical, condemnatory, unforgiving and merciless behaviour. This fruit is evidenced not only in the Pharisees but also in their disciples, for 'a disciple is not above his teacher.' The challenge of this for Jesus' disciples is that they should listen to Him, the true teacher, and so become radically different. As He models to them the kindness and mercy of God (vv. 35-36), so they will begin to bear the fruit of kindness, love, generosity and forgiveness. Conversely, if they insist on sticking with the hypocrisy of the Pharisees, hypocritical fruit will follow. Verse 45 suggests that the issue lies deep within a person's heart. Only a teacher who is able to address and change the heart is worth following – the rest are blind; they will lead to the pit.

### 6:46-69 BUILD YOUR HOUSE WITH AN EYE ON THE FUTURE

As Jesus concludes His 'Sermon on the Plain', He returns to what is a major theme in this Gospel. True discipleship is not simply a matter of *hearing* Jesus' words, but of *acting* upon them. Mary was commended for such an attitude (1:38, 45), but Zechariah was rebuked for its absence (1:20). Later in the Gospel we shall find the same teaching (8:15, 21; 11:27-28). Repeatedly, Luke underlines the importance of acting on Jesus' teaching (3:3; 5:32; 15:7,10; 24:47). In the context of His teaching about true and false teachers, Jesus is here urging His disciples to establish their lives on solid foundations, by listening to His word and by acting upon it. The stream, or flood, in the Bible is indicative of far more than immediate calamity (see Old Testament Notes). Jesus is referring to present, everyday crises as He speaks of the floodwaters, but ultimate and final judgment is in view.

Jesus' manifesto is to 'proclaim good news to the poor' (4:18), to 'forgive sins' (5:24) and to 'call ... sinners to repentance' (5:32). Salvation comes to those who hear His word and act upon it.

## KEY THEMES

+ False teachers and their fruit – Jesus' disciples should avoid false teachers and their judgmental hypocrisy

+ Jesus and His fruit – Jesus' disciples should build their lives on His teaching

## APPLICATION

*To them then:* These verses contain the strongest possible warning against the judgmental hypocrisy that Jesus has encountered from the Pharisees and Teachers of the Law. The context of 5:38 ('new wine must be put into fresh wineskins') and 6:12-16 ('he called his disciples and chose from them twelve, whom he named Apostles') must govern the way we understand the application of Jesus' teaching. Beginning at 6:20, Jesus has been speaking to His disciples, those who will be spurned as evil on account of the Son of Man (6:22). By contrast, the false teachers are well spoken of by all, like the false prophets of old. As Jesus taught His disciples, His intention was to challenge them to follow a true teacher – one who is not blind (v. 39) – so that they will bear good fruit as a result (v. 43).

In these verses Jesus' purpose is not to produce introspective guilt in His listeners, nor endless self-analysis, but to warn them in the strongest possible terms against the false teaching of the religious establishment. He is pointing out to them, forcefully, where such teaching will take them – 'a pit' (v. 39), and 'ruin' (v. 49). Conversely, as Jesus' disciples choose deliberately to break from the false teaching of the 'old wineskins' (5:37), they will bear good fruit. To those who make such a break, future blessing is guaranteed (6:38), good fruit is assured, and their firm foundations will not be shaken on the Day of Judgment. In these verses Jesus' disciples are being encouraged not to indulge in endless self-analysis, but to listen, carefully, attentively and obediently, to His teaching – the fruit will follow.

*To us now:* J. C. Ryle, the famous nineteenth-century Bishop of Liverpool, wrote that 'If a man will hear unsound instruction we cannot expect him to become anything other than unsound in the faith himself… the amount of evil which unsound religious teaching has brought on the church in every age is incalculable'.[1] Our application of these verses should be governed by Jesus' intention. His aim was to warn against the inevitable fruit of false teaching. As true disciples of Jesus submit to His teaching, He will inevitably produce Christ-like godly fruit in them – just as a tree bears fruit, a child carries the DNA of his parents, and a renewed heart produces good treasure (v. 45). Conversely, false teachers will be identifiable both by their own lives and by the lives of their followers. The Apostle Paul warned Timothy about those who had 'the appearance of godliness' but none of its power (2 Tim. 3:5).

---

1.  J. C. Ryle, *Expository Thoughts on the Gospels*, (Exeter: A. Wheaton & Co. Ltd for James Clarke & Co. Ltd 1956), vol. I, p. 189

The purpose of these verses is to challenge Christian disciples to genuine Christ-likeness; the teaching is not designed to produce endless guilt-ridden soul searching. The power of Jesus' teaching and membership of God's family will produce godly fruit in His followers. Application should focus on the seriousness with which we expose ourselves to the teaching of Jesus in the Bible, and also on the importance of not submitting to teachers who refuse to teach the Bible. Both 'blind guides' and 'false prophets' are to be found in the world and the Church. Christ-denying religions and philosophies cut themselves off from the merciful Father and thus produce the ungodly fruit of judgmental hypocrisy. Application should focus on decisions about which church we choose to attend, what teaching we might download from the internet, which books we read, and so forth. We must stress that simply hearing the words of Jesus is not sufficient. Obedient action is required. Repentance is a vital part of the gospel.

## The Aim

The aim of this study is to encourage true disciples of Jesus to build their lives on His teaching and bear godly fruit.

## Suggested Initial Questions

- ✤ Introduction
    - ↘ How did 6:36 summarise Jesus' teaching for the new people of God?
- ✤ 6:37-45
    - ↘ How do verses 37-38 relate to 6:11, 6:22 and 6:26?
    - ↘ Therefore, what should be the attitude of Jesus' disciples towards those who oppose them?
    - ↘ Verses 39-45 are a strong warning against the false teaching of those who oppose Jesus. What is the inevitable result of choosing a bad teacher (vv. 39-40)?
    - ↘ Where does the judgmental hypocrisy of verses 41-42 come from (see vv. 43-45)?
    - ↘ What will be the result of choosing a guide who can see?

↘ By warning His disciples against false teachers (in the context of 6:11, 6:22 and 6:26), what is Jesus seeking to do?

↘ Therefore, what is the key to having the kind of heart that Jesus speaks of in verse 45?

↯ 6:46-49

↘ The 'flood' in the Bible is a picture of God's final judgment (see Old Testament Notes). What is Jesus warning against in these verses?

↘ To 'hear Jesus' words and do them' is a big theme in Luke's Gospel – see 1:38 and 1:45 (Mary) and 1:20 (Zechariah); see also 8:15 and 8:21; 11:29-38. What is the encouragement of these verses?

↘ How does the claim of Jesus in 5:24 and 5:31-32 help deal with our sense of failure as we read the teaching from this and the previous study?

↯ Summary

↘ From this section (4:13–6:49), what have you learned about the mission of Jesus, and about what discipleship will mean for us?

# PART ONE (C)

## LUKE 7 AND 8

# *THE SAVIOUR'S SALVATION*

# Section Notes
# Part One (C): 7 and 8
# The Saviour's Salvation

## How Great a Salvation!

Chapters 7 and 8 of Luke's Gospel form a discrete section whose primary subject is salvation. The chapters contain three major themes: the nature of salvation, the response to salvation and, at the centre of the section, the essence of salvation. The author's aim is that his readers should have certainty concerning the salvation that Jesus, the Saviour, has accomplished.

In the opening verses of his Gospel Luke has made it plain that he desires his readers to have certainty (1:4). As his two-volume work unfolds, Luke clarifies the content of the gospel, demonstrates the credibility of the gospel, and stresses the need for the communication of the gospel. He defines and defends the message of salvation in order that it may be accurately declared.

We should expect to find that the gospel has a precise structure; Luke has indeed written 'an orderly account' (1:3).

Luke should be viewed as a theologian who has organised his material with a purpose: his key pastoral goal is that his readers should be certain about 'the things [they] have been taught' (1:4). It is to achieve this that he has compiled 'a narrative of the things that have been accomplished among us' (1:1).

That chapters 7 and 8 form a discrete section is evident from the section markers in 7:1 and 9:1. The previous section ((4:15–

6:49) records Jesus' public teaching in the synagogues of Galilee. It begins at 4:15 ('And he taught in their synagogues, being glorified by all.') and ends at 7:1 ('After he had finished all his sayings in the hearing of the people …'). The whole section has expounded Jesus' manifesto (4:18-19): He has come to proclaim good news to the poor (4:18). The 'poor' are the people of Israel, and those, like them, under God's judgment. In the book of Isaiah, as we have seen, 'the poor' are synonymous with the spiritually 'blind', 'the captives' and 'the oppressed' in exile (4:18). Jesus' purpose is to forgive people their sin and free them from God's judgment, as can be seen in His action and teaching in chapter 5. He has come, as the Son of Man, with all God's authority – 'on earth' – to declare in the present God's final future verdict of sins forgiven (5:24). 'Poor' sinners, under the judgment of God, are people like the middle-class Peter ('Depart from me, for I am a sinful man' 5:8), the leper ('Lord, If you will, you can make me clean.' 5:12), the paralytic (5:24) and the wealthy Levi (5:27). Jesus has come to summon 'sinners to repentance' (5:32).

Therefore, Jesus' manifesto, viewed in both its immediate and its wider biblical context, has precious little to do with economics, fair trade, environmental action or medical aid. It has everything to do with rescuing men and women from their own sin and from God's judgment. It has always been God's purpose to rescue every class of humanity from sin and wrath. His grace extends to Gentiles as well as Jews, and poor people like the widow of Zarephath (4:26) as well as prominent people like Naaman, the high-class Syrian General (4:27).

In the following section (9:1-50) Jesus is identified as 'the Christ of God' by Peter (9:20) and as 'my Son, my Chosen One' at His transfiguration (9:35). Jesus insists that 'the Son of Man must suffer many things and be rejected … and be killed, and on the third day be raised.' (9:22) Jesus' words are confirmed by Moses and Elijah (representing the Law and the Prophets) who discuss with Him 'his departure, which he was about to accomplish at Jerusalem.' (9:31) At the heart of this section is a summons by Jesus to discipleship: 'If anyone would come after me, let him deny himself, take up his cross daily and follow me.' (9:23)

The subject matter of chapters 7 and 8 follows on logically from chapters 4 – 6. The contention is that Dr Luke has so organised his material as to provide a 'module' on salvation, so that his readers will be certain about the nature of the salvation that Jesus has come to bring, certain about the wrong and the right response to this salvation, and certain about the essence of this salvation: how great a salvation!

## THE SUBJECT

Salvation is the principal subject of the section, which begins and ends with miracles of salvation: the centurion's servant is healed, the widow's son is raised from the dead, the storm is calmed, the demoniac is restored, and Jairus' daughter and the woman with bleeding are saved.

When John the Baptist questions Jesus' identity (7:19-20), Jesus responds by quoting Isaiah 35:6,7. According to Isaiah, the great Saviour of God's people will bring release from all that spoils this sin-wrecked world, suffering as it does under the deserved wrath of God. The Saviour will lead His people on the highway of salvation. 'He will come and save you.' (Isa. 35:4) Thus Jesus views His miracles as eschatological thunderbolts, providing evidence for His glorious salvation and also a foretaste of it.

This is confirmed by Luke's unique use of the word 'to save' in 7:3, 7:50, 8:12, 8:36, 8:50. In these verses Luke uses the word 'to save' where, in the equivalent incidents in other Gospels, no mention of salvation is given. The Greek word 'save' can, of course, mean 'heal', and it is often translated as such (7:3, 8:36), but it cannot mean 'heal' in 7:50. Jesus uses precisely the same words to the sinful woman (7:50) as He does to the woman with bleeding (8:48). This indicates that when Luke uses the word in these chapters, he is describing aspects of the salvation that Jesus has come to bring.[1]

---

1. Gooding, ibid., pp. 126-7

## Key Themes

Chapters 7 and 8 contain three key themes: salvation, responses to salvation, and the essence of salvation.

The section begins and ends with miracles of salvation. These miracles show Jesus to be the redeeming Saviour of Isaiah 35. They are evidence that the new Age of Salvation has begun with His arrival. They are 'pictures' of salvation. Like the show house on a building site, these miracles give a snapshot of the future. Disease (the centurion's servant), death (the widow of Nain's son), disordered creation (the calming of the storm), the devil himself (the demoniac) – all of these are evidence of a fallen world that is under the judgment of God. In chapter 8 the account of the healing, of both Jairus' daughter and the woman with bleeding, contains a summary of the whole section; the key point of these two chapters is contained in Jesus' words to the woman, 'Daughter, your faith has saved you [made you well]; go in peace.' (8:48)

In chapter 7, following the first two miracles, Jesus explains who He is and also why some are responding negatively to Him (7:18-35). The evidence for His identity is consistent. Both Isaiah (chapter 35) and the Baptist confirm it (7:24-28). Those who reject Him do so not through lack of evidence, but through hardness of heart. They had not 'been baptised by him [John]', and they had refused to repent (7:29-30). Their rejection of salvation is moral, not intellectual, and Jesus Himself condemns them as being like contrary children in the playground, who refuse to come out to dance, no matter what music is offered (7:31-32).

After the story of the sinful woman, Jesus' parables lay out the positive response that is expected (8:1-21). 'As for that in the good soil, they are those who, hearing the word, hold it fast in an honest and good heart, and bear fruit with patience.' (8:15) What matters is holding on to God's word and obeying it: Jesus said to the crowd, 'My mother and my brothers are those who hear the word of God and do it.' (8:21)

At the centre of this section, Luke has placed the story of the sinful woman (7:36-50). The contrast between the woman and

Simon the Pharisee is stark. 'The Pharisee' (7:36, 37, 39) is self-righteous and, having invited the King of kings into his house, fails to treat him with even a modicum of the respect that is due. The woman, conversely, has been forgiven much.[2] This woman, then, is the personification of the poor sinner for whom Jesus has come. Having put her faith in Jesus, she has provided the model response: 'Your faith has saved you; go in peace.' (7:50, cf. 8:48)

## THE STRUCTURE OF CHAPTERS 7 AND 8

The structure of the section, then, works as follows:

| | |
|---|---|
| 7:1-17 | Two salvation miracles |
| 7:18-35 | Response to Jesus' salvation |
| 7:36-50 | The essence of salvation: "Your faith has saved you; go in peace." |
| 8:1-21 | Response to Jesus' salvation |
| 8:22-39 | Two salvation miracles |
| 8:40-56 | Conclusion: 'Your faith has saved you; go in peace.' |

## APPLICATION

A number of important applications emerge.

First, salvation is ultimately eschatological, that is, it will be revealed fully at the end of time when this world order is brought to a close. Then, God will reveal Jesus' final and absolute rescue of humanity from disease, death, disorder in creation, and the devil himself. Jesus is the one who will accomplish this rescue on that day, and His miracles were performed to show this. These great enemies afflict all humanity, and humanity, in spite of its God-given ingenuity, has no answer to the consequences of the Fall. The gospel of the Lord Jesus Christ alone provides an answer to our bondage to decay. Jesus Christ alone has defeated sin and death, and He summons men and women onto the highway of the redeemed.

---

2. The ESV has the translation 'are forgiven' in verse 47 and verse 48. It is equally possible to translate the verb as 'have been forgiven'; her love was the result of her forgiveness.

Too frequently our Jesus is too small: we have failed to understand the immeasurable impact of human sinfulness, and thus to appreciate the cosmic scale of Jesus' salvation. A 'dinky toy' Jesus with a matchbox salvation will have little relevance to the world. Other agendas will be manufactured in order to make Him more relevant. Some in the church will emphasise a social gospel – the alleviation of poverty; redeeming the city; environmental action. Others will emphasise a happy life; love; joy. Conversely, the Great Salvation presented in Luke chapters 7 and 8 requires little contextualisation or indigenisation. The effects of sin and judgment are known and felt by everyone the world over.

Secondly, the protestations of those who reject Jesus are shown for what they are. Rejection of Christ stems from a moral refusal to repent, not an intellectual failure to be convinced. Contrary games are played in order to avoid Christ's demands. He sees straight through them. The figures of the Pharisee and the lawyer, in the Gospels, should not be identified, in the first instance, with the believing congregation. The direct line of application is to the unbelieving pagan – whether a religious Jew, an imam, or a fundamentalist secularist. The evidence for the identity of Christ and His salvation is entirely logical and consistent. The unbelievers' rejection of this evidence shows them for what they are, and Christ for who He is – 'Yet wisdom is justified by all her children.' (See Text Notes for 7:35) The right response to Christ is to hold fast to His word and to persevere.

Thirdly, salvation is by grace, through faith in Christ. Salvation comes immediately to the sinful woman; Jesus declares her to be at peace with God. Just as the judgment of the last day is pronounced (in the present) over the paralytic (5:24), so she is declared to be now at peace with God. This is consistent with all of Luke's account (1:76-79; 24:47). The sin-bearing, wrath-satisfying death of Jesus, and the personal response of the individual sinner (cf. 8:48; 17:19; 19:9-10; 24:46-47), is at the heart of this Great Salvation. Thus, the doctrine of this Gospel is at one with the doctrine of the epistles and, indeed, with the doctrine of the whole Bible. Entry into the

Great Salvation comes for free as, one by one, men and women put their trust in Jesus (Gen. 15:6; Luke 19:10).

## C ONCLUSION

This study, on a section of Luke's Gospel, prompts one final comment for the Christian preacher concerning his task. The primary task of the Christian preacher is not, first and foremost, to act as 'the theologian', or indeed to lean on the theology of one or another great one from years gone by. The task of the Christian preacher is to listen to, and be shaped by, the theology of the Bible writers and the way they have applied that theology. *They* are the theologians, and it is *their* word that pastors the congregation. Insofar as the preacher yields to the author's intent and purpose, both theologically and pastorally, so far will his preaching cut with the grain of the text and thus carry the weight of God's word. God's voice will be heard; God's work will be done. But insofar as he places his confidence in relevance, thorough cultural engagement, or power through the presentation of another's theological grid, so far will his proclamation be weightless, on the one hand, or predictable (or simply wrong) on the other.

# The Saviour's Great Salvation
# Luke 7:1-35

## THE CONTEXT

Jesus of Nazareth has been presented by Luke as 'a Savior, who is Christ the Lord.' (2:11) Luke's stated aim is his readers' certainty 'concerning the things [they] have been taught.' (1:4) In Luke's Gospel this certainty has been built up, firstly, by his defence of the historical, theological and 'political' credentials of the gospel. Secondly, he has encouraged his readers' certainty by defining the content of the gospel. This confidence in the gospel's credibility and its content is intended to result in the good news of salvation being declared to all nations (24:47).

So far Luke has laid out Jesus' CV (1:5–4:13) and also His manifesto (4:14–6:49). Chapter 7 begins a new section of the gospel, which extends to 8:56. The issue at stake in these chapters is made clear as Jesus answers John the Baptist's question in 7:19. Jesus responds to the question about His own identity with language that recalls Isaiah's prophecy of God's long-promised salvation. Luke's aim in chapters 7 and 8 is to clarify for his readers the nature of the salvation that Jesus of Nazareth has come to bring.

## THE STRUCTURE

7:1-17      Two miracles of salvation: Jesus saves from disease and death

*7:18-35*    Responding to the Saviour's salvation

## OLD TESTAMENT NOTES

*Elijah and Elisha:* Both Elijah and Elisha were prophets whose authority was confirmed by a miracle: the raising from death of a woman's only son (1 Kings 17:17-24; 2 Kings 4:18-37).

*Isaiah 35:1-10:* Through Isaiah, God promised salvation to His people. His redeemed people were to return from exile with songs of everlasting joy (35:10), along the highway of holiness (35:8). This highway is depicted as a triumphal procession to salvation. It leads to a place from which all the effects of God's judgment at human sin have been removed forever (35:5-7). These promises of salvation, or rescue, from disease, death, disorder and the devil, have been repeated through Isaiah's prophesy (25:6-12; 26:19). They culminate in God's promise of a New Creation (65:17). Earlier, Isaiah's prophecy had included a warning for those who harden their hearts and are offended by the Lord and His salvation (8:14).

*Malachi 3:1:* Through Malachi, God had promised a messenger, who would herald His coming in person to save.

## TEXT NOTES

### 7:1-17 TWO MIRACLES OF SALVATION

Verse 1 indicates a new section of the gospel. In verses 1-17 Luke records two miracles. When, in 7:19, the disciples of John the Baptist ask whether Jesus is 'the one who is to come', Jesus responds with immediate action (7:21), healing many and restoring sight to the blind. He refers John the Baptist to the promises God made to Isaiah (see Old Testament Notes). This provides a grid of understanding for the healing miracles. These are intended to demonstrate that Jesus is the long-promised Saviour who has come to bring, ultimately, God's promised New Creation. He has power to save and to summon the redeemed to be led on the highway of salvation (see Old Testament Notes). H. K. Nielson comments: '... these healings are signs of the presence of the Kingdom of God (expressions of its reality) in the same way that snowdrops are signs of Spring.'[1] Jesus' miracles, then, are both evidence for, and a foretaste of, the kingdom He has come to bring.

*vv1-10 Jesus saves from disease:* Jesus has the power to save from disease. A centurion in the occupying Roman army was a man of considerable power. He was the equivalent of a major in the military of today. His command of over 100 men was for the purpose of maintaining law and order in the region for which he was responsible. Luke, the doctor, provides a medical note of the servant's condition (v. 2), and considerable detail on the centurion's character. He was clearly a decent, God-fearing man. The servant was legally his possession – but he valued him highly. The Gentile centurion's community work showed an unusual care for God's people (vv. 3-5). Furthermore, the centurion showed humility towards Jesus over whom, technically, he had absolute authority (v. 6). With his power delegated from Rome, the centurion was used to exercising unquestioned authority. When he spoke it was as if Tiberius himself were speaking. As a man of power he recognised absolute power when he saw it; he knew that Jesus needed only to speak in order to 'save' his servant. The Greek word for 'heal' in verse 3 is literally 'save'; the use of this Greek word at this point confirms the theme of the whole section. Jesus' astonishment at the faith of the centurion, and His commendation of it, indicate not only the breadth of the salvation that He had come to bring, but also that He accepted the centurion's recognition of His divine authority. He has indeed come to save, and even Gentiles will benefit from His salvation.

*vv11-17 Jesus saves from death:* In a society with no social welfare beyond that of the family, a widow's only son was her sole means of support. The widow of Nain's situation was desperate. Luke provides characteristic narrative detail: 'a great crowd' … 'near to the gate' … 'a considerable crowd from the town' … 'he touched the bier'. While Luke emphasises the compassion of Jesus (v. 13), the fact remains that His actions – commanding the woman not

---

1.   John Nolland, *Luke* (Word Biblical Commentary), (Dallas, Texas: World Publishing 1989), p. 641

to weep, touching the coffin, and speaking to the corpse – would have been utterly callous, if He had not the authority to deliver. But He did have the authority to raise the dead, and so the response of the crowd, reminiscent of Zechariah's words (1:78), is an apt commentary on the incident. God has come to save.

7:18-35 RESPONDING TO THE SAVIOUR'S SALVATION

These verses form one of two passages in this section which focus on the response to the Saviour's salvation (see *The Structure of Chapters 7 and 8* in the Section Notes for these chapters). Verses 18-35 break into three parts: verses 18-23 'Identifying the Saviour', verses 24-30 'Responding to the Baptist', and verses 31-35 'Weighing the response'. Luke takes us to the heart of the matter with his narrator's comment in verses 29-30. Rejection of Jesus has little to do with a lack of evidence and everything to do with a refusal to repent. It is primarily a moral, not an intellectual matter.

*vv18-23 Identifying the Saviour:* John the Baptist's question in verse 19, repeated in verse 20, and Jesus' immediate action and reply (vv. 21-23), indicate the scale of Jesus' claims. Isaiah had promised a New Creation and a Saviour who would summon the redeemed for salvation (see Old Testament Notes). Jesus self-consciously accepts this role. He acts 'in that hour' (v. 21) and then answers the Baptist with a combination of verses from Isaiah, all of which speak of the coming Saviour. Isaiah had anticipated that some people would be scandalised by God's Saviour (Isa. 8:14); Jesus promises God's favour for those who are not offended by Him. His use of the word 'me' in verse 23 would show extraordinary arrogance if He were not who He claims to be.

*vv24-30 Responding to the Baptist:* Jesus substantiates His claim to be the Saviour by means of a commentary on the ministry of John the Baptist. The Baptist was introduced in Luke's Gospel as the promised prophet, like Elijah, who would 'make ready for the Lord a people prepared.' (1:17) He was to 'go before the Lord to prepare his ways' (1:76). The Baptist was neither a weak man nor a soft man. He was not a crowd-pleaser, tailoring his message to suit his audience, blowing this way and that in the wind (v. 24).

Nor was he a pawn in the pocket of the political establishment, saying only what was acceptable to his paymasters (v. 25). Rather, the Baptist was an authentic prophet from God, speaking the word of God. Jesus' use of Malachi 3:1 (v. 27) adds more weight to His claim to divinity and authority. Malachi had promised a messenger who would 'prepare the way before me [the Lord].' (See Old Testament Notes.) This explains verse 28: if the Baptist was indeed the one promised by Malachi, then the kingdom of God had broken into the world with the arrival of God as King. Those who accepted the Baptist's message, and recognised Jesus as their King, had access to everything that the Baptist's ministry anticipated.

Verses 29-30 explain why some accepted and others rejected the message of the Baptist and the ministry of Jesus. It all hung on whether or not they had been 'baptised with the baptism of John.' John's baptism was 'a baptism of repentance for the forgiveness of sins.' (3:3) The reason the Pharisees and teachers of the Law rejected Jesus had little to do with the presence or absence of evidence, and everything to do with a refusal to repent. The tax collectors and people who did recognise Jesus did so because they were prepared to repent.

*vv31-35 Weighing the response:* Jesus' analysis of those who rejected Him portrays them as what they were: contrary and unwilling to be satisfied by *any* evidence. He compares them to children who, when summoned, refuse to come out to play. When wedding music is played, they won't dance because, they say, they want to play 'funerals'. When those who wish to play with them change the tune and play funeral music, they immediately insist they won't play because they want to play 'weddings'. The Pharisees and Scribes who refuse to listen to the voice of God are just like them. When the Baptist came like a prophet of old, with God's command to repent, they refused and instead accused him of demon-possession. When Jesus arrived offering salvation and demonstrating His power to save, they accused Him of being a glutton and drunkard. Verse 35 seems hard to understand until it is read in its context. The children of wisdom are those who respond rightly to the truth. Their lack of hypocrisy, as they weigh the evidence and obey the voice of God, is itself proof that what Jesus and John the Baptist are teaching is from God; Jesus' teaching produces the 'fruit' of which He spoke earlier (6:43-44). Chapter 7:36-50 will provide a commentary on this verse.

## KEY THEMES

- Salvation: Jesus saves from disease and death

- Identity: Jesus is the Saviour come to bring God's long-promised Great Salvation

- Response: people's acceptance or rejection of Jesus turns on a willingness to repent

## APPLICATION

*To them then:* The people of Jesus' day were waiting for a Saviour, promised by God, who would rescue from sickness, disease, death and the effects of the Fall. John the Baptist's question (verse 19) and Jesus' response indicate that He is that Saviour. This shows how the crowds were meant to understand and interpret the two miracles of verses 1-17. They are miracles of salvation intended to identify Jesus as the Saviour. The centurion, though a Gentile, recognised Jesus' authority to save. The great crowd at Nain acknowledged that God had 'visited his people.' Jesus was demonstrating that He is the one who will rescue God's people from this fallen world and lead them on the highway of salvation. His rescue will involve, ultimately, salvation from disease and death. As Isaiah had promised (and Zechariah had recognised in the Temple, chapter 2:32), Gentiles were to benefit from Jesus' saving work. Not everybody was prepared to acknowledge Jesus for who He was. Jesus explains why. There is no lack of evidence, nor an absence of God's word. Jesus' miracles spoke for themselves, and no one could deny that John the Baptist was a prophet from God. Rather, the Pharisees and teachers of the Law would not accept Jesus because they would not recognise themselves as sinners, and so repent. Their hard-heartedness manifested itself in a contrary, hypocritical treatment of the evidence. One minute they would ask for one thing and then, when it was provided, they would immediately change their tune and demand something else. They would not believe because they would not repent.

*To us now:* It is easy to under-represent the scale of the salvation that Jesus has come to bring. The two healing miracles demonstrate that Jesus' salvation will ultimately extend to a rescue from everything that spoils this fallen world. While we must be careful not to draw a direct line from individual sin to individual suffering (see 13:1-5), the Bible is clear, nonetheless, that disease, death, disorder and the presence of evil all come as a result of the Fall. In verses 1-17 Jesus demonstrates that He Himself has all God's power to rescue humanity from all of these things. His salvation is available to the Gentiles (like the centurion) and to the dispossessed (like the widow). Not only does He have compassion on the lost, He has the power to do something about it. These miracles show Jesus' salvation to be far bigger and more far-reaching than it is often presented as being. Jesus has not come simply to 'make my life a bit better', to be my 'special friend', or to provide 'wish-fulfilment' for His disciples. He has come to overthrow the horrendous effects of the Fall, to redeem His people, and to lead them on the highway of salvation towards His New Creation. Not only does He claim to have come for this purpose, He has demonstrated that He has the power to deliver. The idea that Luke, a medical doctor, might have made up or been fooled into exaggerating the incidents he records is absurd. He knew that dead people do not rise!

The question remains as to why some refuse to accept Jesus' salvation. Jesus exposes the hearts of those who reject Him. It is simply not the case that there is insufficient evidence; His opponents have the evidence of both the Baptist's testimony and Jesus' recent miracles. The issue at stake is not a lack of proof, but a refusal to repent. The twenty-first century equivalent of the Pharisees and

149

lawyers are those who refuse to take the evidence seriously, and instead seek to hide behind a variety of excuses. Whether it's the celebrity atheist, members of the religious Establishment, the friend in the pub or the family member, Jesus can see straight through their contrary hypocrisy. He knows that the issue is not one of intellect, but of will. They reject the purposes of God because they will not accept the baptism of John; in other words, they will not repent. The issue is moral, not intellectual.

## THE AIM

The aim of this study is to see the scale of Jesus' salvation, and to understand why people refuse to accept the salvation He offers.

## SUGGESTED INITIAL QUESTIONS

- ✤ Introduction
  - ↘ From what Luke has told us so far, what is the main purpose of Jesus' work? (See 1:47; 1:77; 2:11; 4:18; 5:24; 5:32.)
- ✤ 7:1-10
  - ↘ How does verse 1 indicate the start of a new section?
  - ↘ What do verses 2-10 teach us about who, from what, and how Jesus has come to save?
- ✤ 7:11-17
  - ↘ What do verses 11-17 teach us about who, from what, and how Jesus has come to save?
- ✤ 7:18-35
  - ↘ 7:18-23

    Look up Isaiah 35:5-10. What does God promise through the prophet Isaiah in these verses?

    What, then, is John the Baptist asking in Luke 7:19?

    How do Jesus' actions and words (vv. 21-23) answer John the Baptist's question?
  - ↘ 7:24-28

    What kind of man was John the Baptist?

    How does the prophet Malachi help us understand the Baptist?

↘ 7:29-35

How do Jesus' words in verses 29-30 help explain both why people accept Jesus and why they reject Him? (NB: What did the baptism of John represent? (3:3))

How do the contrary children in Jesus' illustration (vv. 31-32) shed light on how people responded to God's word, through the Baptist and through Jesus?

How does this make sense of the way people respond today?

✤ Summary

↘ How do these verses build confidence in Jesus?

# The Essence of Salvation
## Luke 7:36-50

## The Context

Salvation has been established as the key theme of this section of Luke's Gospel (7:1–8:56). On being asked by the Baptist, 'Are you the one who is to come, or shall we look for another?', Jesus has healed many people and restored the sight of many who were blind. In this way, and in His answer to the question, Jesus has presented Himself as the long-promised Saviour. He has come to summon the redeemed and to lead them on the highway of salvation. The healing miracles (7:1-17) are thus rightly understood to be evidence of the salvation that Jesus has come to bring. His great saving work will ultimately involve the defeat of disease and death. He is saving His people for His New Creation. Luke's presentation of this great salvation was followed by Jesus' verdict on those who accepted Him and also those who rejected Him. Negative responses to Jesus were explained as being the result not of insufficient evidence, but of an unwillingness to repent. Those who accepted the salvation He offered were doing so not only on the basis of His works of salvation, but also on the basis of the Baptist's summons to repent.

Luke follows this analysis with the account of the sinful woman in Simon the Pharisee's house. This takes the reader to the very heart of the matter. Salvation is received by grace, through faith, in

Christ. The responses of the sinful woman and of Simon are both examples of verse 35. One is a child of wisdom, the other is not.

## The Structure

| | |
|---|---|
| 7:36 | Introduction: Jesus at the Pharisee's table |
| 7:37-39 | The sinful woman and Simon the Pharisee: gratitude and grumbling |
| 7:40-43 | The explanatory parable: grace and gratitude |
| 7:44-48 | Simon and the sinful woman: grumbling and gratitude |
| 7:49-50 | Conclusion: at the Pharisee's table – salvation, by grace, through faith |

## Old Testament Notes

There is no direct reference to the Old Testament in these verses. However, the whole incident is set in the context of the customs and norms of Old Testament hospitality.

## Text Notes

### 7:36 Introduction: Jesus at the Pharisee's table

The setting of these verses is a meal laid on for Jesus by Simon the Pharisee. Luke is at pains to stress that the host is a Pharisee. He mentions it twice in verse 36 and twice more in verses 37-39. Table fellowship expressed closeness and intimacy. The Pharisee had invited Jesus into the heart of his social circle. However, these references to 'the Pharisee' in the context of 7:30; 6:24-26; 6:11 and 5:30 are designed to alert the reader to potential conflict.

### 7:37-39 The sinful woman and Simon the Pharisee: gratitude and grumbling

Luke does not record details of the sinful woman's sin. The reader should not speculate. She was, however, publicly known as 'a sinner' (vv. 37 and 39). Jesus 'was reclining at table' – the table would have been low, about the height of a bench, and guests lay down to eat at the 'tricilium', propping themselves on cushions and rests. Their feet extended outwards from the table. For a woman to show her hair in public was considered by the religious to be improper and immodest. The most devout did not even let down their hair in front of their family. The sinful woman's action in verse 38 broke all social conventions and would have shocked the religious Simon and his guests. An 'alabaster flask of ointment' was a commodity of considerable value – probably an heirloom. Luke repeats his note that Jesus had been invited by the Pharisee to his house (v. 39). The Pharisee takes exception to Jesus' toleration of the sinful woman and, like the Pharisees we find in chapters 4:14–6:49, he uses Jesus' acceptance of the 'sinner' to question Jesus' identity.

### 7:40-43 THE EXPLANATORY PARABLE: GRACE AND GRATITUDE

A denarius was the equivalent of a day's wages for an unskilled labourer. One debtor had debts written off ten times that of the other. The question Jesus asks has an obvious answer – Simon provides it.

### 7:44-48 SIMON AND THE SINFUL WOMAN: GRUMBLING AND GRATITUDE

Jesus now applies the parable to Simon and the sinful woman. Simon, though host to Jesus, had failed even in the most basic social niceties of the day. It was *de rigueur* in polite Jewish society to wash a visitor's feet. People walked either barefoot or in open-toed sandals. In a pre-mechanised society where animals provided transport the streets were filled with filth. Feet needed washing. Guests were to be greeted with an embrace and with oil for the anointing of the head. Simon had provided none of these. His failure was, at least, a snub to his guest. The offence was multiplied in proportion to the significance of his guest. In entertaining Jesus he had opened his home to 'a Saviour, who is Christ the Lord.' (2:11) Jesus was a major religious figure and had been identified as such not only by John the Baptist but also by the vast crowds who followed him. It seems, however, that Simon's invitation to Jesus was yet another attempt by the Pharisees to ensnare Him (see 6:7) and had been extended with grudging reluctance.

On the other hand, the sinful woman had provided in abundance at every point where Simon had failed. She had cast social custom to the wind and, in an uninhibited display of gratitude, had embraced and anointed Jesus' dirty feet.

Verse 47 explains the woman's action. The words 'are forgiven' are in the past tense and could equally be translated 'have been forgiven' (see the New American Standard Bible translation). Jesus' point is not that her display of devotion had earned her forgiveness, but that gratitude for her forgiveness had prompted this display of devotion. The contrast between the Pharisee, who saw no need for repentance and forgiveness of sin (5:32; 7:30), and the sinful woman could not have been more marked. The one was out to trap Jesus and sought to snub Him even as he hypocritically welcomed Him into his home. The other expressed unrestrained thanksgiving – regardless of the opinion of others. Where the woman had heard of Jesus' offer of forgiveness we are not told. The incident appears to have taken place in the region of Capernaum (7:1). She might have been present to hear His proclamation of the gospel at any of the occasions mentioned in Luke 4:14 – 6:49 (4:31, 42-44; 5:1-3 etc.). She is certainly a typical example of the 'poor' to whom Jesus proclaimed the good news (4:18; 7:22).

7:49-50 Conclusion: at the Pharisee's table – salvation, by grace, through faith.

The table guests' question echoes the Pharisees' complaint in 5:21. Only God has authority to forgive sins – so who is this? Jesus' words to the woman take the reader to the very heart of His offer of salvation. They explain how it is that the great salvation He has come to bring is made available to individual members of His Kingdom. Salvation is to come through faith alone – 'Your faith has saved you'. Salvation is to come through Jesus – He is at the centre of the whole incident. Salvation is on the basis of grace – she had no works of her own. Salvation is 'peace' with God.

The peace promised by Jesus in Luke's Gospel is not a promise of an immediate end to political unrest. Jesus assures His followers that 'Nation will rise against nation …' (21:10). Nor does it suggest universally restored relationships in this age. Jesus says, 'Do you think that I have come to give peace on earth? No, I tell you, but rather division.' (12:51) Instead, the "peace' on offer is a restored relationship with God the Father, which comes as a result of the forgiveness of sins (1:76-79). This is how Jesus will 'guide our feet into the way of peace.' (1:79) Thus salvation comes through faith in Christ, and faith is the means by which an individual steps onto the 'highway of holiness' which we have seen is the road of salvation. Such an individual is assured, ultimately, of a place in the New Creation which Jesus has come to bring.

## KEY THEMES

Salvation:

+ comes by grace through faith

+ is available in Christ

+ comes through the forgiveness of sins

+ is available even to the notorious sinner

+ will result in gratitude

+ is offensive to those who have no awareness of personal guilt

## APPLICATION

*To them then:* The purpose of this incident is to provide a 'worked example' of Jesus' teaching in 7:29-35. The Pharisee has little awareness of his own sin and thus no sense of his need for forgiveness. He is clearly not someone who has been 'baptised with the baptism of John'. He places little to no value on Jesus. Indeed, Simon deliberately snubs Jesus, failing to show even the most basic social courtesy to his 'celebrity guest'. Simon is typical of the Pharisees and appears intent on trapping Jesus even as he offers Him hospitality. In 7:35 Jesus stated that 'wisdom is justified by all her children.' Simon's response to Jesus demonstrates his heart – he is a self-righteous hypocrite.

Conversely, the sinful woman's attitude to Jesus is an accurate barometer of her heart. She is a notorious sinner and she knows it. Her self-awareness results in her placing the highest value on Jesus' offer of forgiveness. She is saved by grace, through faith in Christ. The table guests at Simon's house recognise the significance of Jesus' pronouncement. The words 'Your sins are forgiven' have been spoken by Jesus previously (5:20). On that occasion they provoked a similar response (5:21). Jesus reiterates His offer to the sinful woman and thereby indicates the means by which salvation comes to an individual. His statement 'Your faith has saved you; go in peace' takes His listeners to the heart of the gospel. He has come to bring peace with God (2:14), which is salvation. Salvation comes by grace, through faith in Christ.

*To us now*: This incident lies right at the heart of this section of Luke's Gospel (see *The Structure of Chapters 7 and 8* in the Section Notes for these chapters). The issue at stake in the section is the great salvation that Jesus has come to bring. He is the Saviour of Isaiah 35 who has come to redeem and to summon and lead the redeemed on the highway of salvation. This salvation will involve, ultimately, the restoration of everything lost at the Fall – it will be a New Creation. By placing this incident at the heart of the section Luke indicates how an individual sets foot on the road to salvation. It is by grace, through faith in Christ. The forgiveness of an individual's sins lies at the heart of salvation. The sinful woman is the 'poor' person to whom Jesus came to proclaim good news (4:18; 7:22). She is the 'sick' person who needs 'a physician' (5:31). Salvation is on offer to any poor sinner who is prepared to hear Jesus' summons to repent and believe. Awareness of the magnitude of personal sin, and the extent of the salvation Jesus offers, will produce in us unadulterated gratitude. Conversely, when people are convinced of their own personal righteousness they will not respond to Jesus – Jesus has 'not come to call the righteous but sinners to repentance.' (5:32) Those who are righteous in their own eyes will not benefit from Jesus' salvation.

## THE AIM

The aim of this study is that we should learn to love Christ for the salvation that comes by faith alone through grace alone.

## SUGGESTED INITIAL QUESTIONS

✥ Introduction

   ↘ What did we learn in the last study about the great salvation that Jesus has come to bring?

   ↘ What did we learn about the reason why some people accept Jesus and others reject Him?

✥ 7:36-39

   ↘ What do verses 36-39 tell us about the key players in this incident?

   ↘ What do we already know about the Pharisees? (5:30; 6:2, 11)

✥ 7:40-48

   ↘ Why does Jesus commend Simon for the answer he gives in verse 43?

   ↘ How did Simon's behaviour towards Jesus reveal his heart towards Him?

   ↘ The words translated as 'are forgiven' in verses 47 and 48 could equally be translated as 'have been forgiven'. What difference would that make?

   ↘ How does Jesus' explanation make sense of the woman's behaviour?

   ↘ What does this reveal about the hearts of the people Jesus spoke about in verses 31-32?

   ↘ What does this reveal about our hearts as we seek to follow Jesus?

✥ 7:49-50

   ↘ Jesus' words to the woman in verse 50 are repeated exactly in 8:48; they reflect Zechariah's words (1:77), the Baptist's message (3:3) and Jesus' mission (5:24, 32). What does this tell us about the essence of the salvation that Jesus has come to bring? (Who is it for? How is it received? From where does it come? What does it result in?)

↳ Summary

    ↘ This incident lies at the centre of this section of Luke's Gospel. What did we learn in the last study (7:1-35) about the salvation that Jesus has come to bring?

    ↘ What does the teaching in this incident add?

# Responding to the Saviour's Salvation
## Luke 8:1-21

## THE CONTEXT

Luke's purpose in this section of his Gospel (7:1–8:56) has been to define the extent of the great salvation that the Saviour has come to bring (7:1-17), the right response to it (7:18-35), and the essence of it (7:36-50). Luke wants his readers to be certain about the content of salvation. He has shown that Jesus has the power, as the long-awaited Saviour, to usher in His New Creation – He has authority over disease and death (7:1-17). Luke has also demonstrated why some people respond positively and others negatively to this offer of salvation. The issue is not to do with a lack of evidence but rather an unwillingness to repent. Then, the incident with the sinful woman in Simon the Pharisee's house has shown what is the essence of salvation: an individual is saved by grace through faith in Christ (7:48-50).

Luke now returns to the theme of what is the right response to the great salvation that Jesus has come to bring (see *The Structure of Chapters 7 and 8* in the Section Notes for these chapters). The issue at stake is 'hearing'.

## THE STRUCTURE

Responding rightly to Jesus' Great Salvation:

| 8:1-3 | Jesus' close followers |
|---|---|
| 8:4-8 | The parable of the sower – 'He who has ears to hear, let him hear.' |
| 8:9-15 | The parable explained – 'Hear the word and hold it fast!' |
| 8:16-18 | The parable of the lamp – 'Take care then how you hear...' |
| 8:19-21 | Jesus' close family – '... are those who hear the word of God and do it.' |

## Old Testament Notes

'*Keep on hearing, but do not understand*' (*Isaiah 6:9*): In Isaiah 6, after five chapters in which Israel's rebellion against God has been detailed, God calls Isaiah. Isaiah's commission is to speak God's word to God's people. However, God's message through Isaiah is initially one of judgment: as a result of Israel's sin God was going to blind the eyes of His people to Isaiah's message, to block their ears and make their hearts unresponsive. It is important to note that the 'blinding' (in Isaiah 6) should be understood in the context of the sin described in chapters 1–5. God is not acting pre-emptively; the blinding is a consequence of Israel's sin, not its cause.

## Text Notes

### 8:1-3 Jesus' close followers

Luke introduces these verses, which will be about the right response to the great salvation Jesus has come to bring, with a reminder of Jesus' priority in preaching the word of the Kingdom of God, and then a detailed record of some who were His closest followers. Jesus is about to teach that the right response to His offer of salvation is to hear His word and obey it. Those who do this will be closer to Him than His closest family (8:21). Verses 1-3 introduce the key theme of the study. Verse one indicates that Jesus was continuing to pursue the priority He had set in 4:18 and 4:42-44. Verses 2-3 contain characteristic Lukan detail concerning individual disciples, each of whom would have been identifiable by his early readers. The diversity of background of these individuals indicates the social breadth of Jesus' early followers.

8:4-8 THE PARABLE OF THE SOWER – 'HE WHO HAS EARS TO HEAR, LET HIM HEAR.'

Great crowds were increasingly becoming a feature of Jesus' public ministry (5:1, 15; 6:17; 7:11). He teaches them in parables and uses agricultural imagery. Prior to the invention of precision drilling, cultivation involved the broadcasting of seed. The seed was carried in a shoulder bag and scattered by hand. Inevitably there would be considerable wastage as seed fell on unprepared soil, poor land, or untended parts of the field. Scavenging birds accounted for the loss of some seed, shallow soil and rocky outcrops for more, and unkempt patches at the margin of the field for still more. However, seed falling on good soil yielded a bumper harvest. This parable, told to the crowd, came with a command: listen!

8:9-15 THE PARABLE EXPLAINED – 'HEAR THE WORD AND HOLD IT FAST!'

Jesus' explanation of His parable was only provided for His disciples. It draws on Isaiah 6 (see Old Testament Notes). The parables contain truth from God, but Jesus' presentation of the truth was deliberately oblique. The reason for this is explained by Isaiah 6. God's truth was preached by Isaiah, together with the offer of salvation. However, God obscured the meaning for those who had rejected Him, while at the same time making it plain to others. Jesus understood His preaching ministry to operate in the same way. This means that His disciples should expect a mixed response to the proclamation of the gospel, depending on the soil of human hearts into which God's word is being planted. His word is the seed (v. 11), which is scattered far and wide. One aspect of the mixed response to the gospel is that Satan, the scavenger, snatches away the word from the heart of some (v. 12).

This parable is also recorded by Matthew and Mark, but only Luke includes the phrase 'and be saved' (v. 12), which provides further evidence that the key theme of this section (chapters 7 and 8) is salvation. The mixed response will also mean that some people appear to show signs of early growth. These people will receive the word with joy (v. 13). In Luke's Gospel and also Acts, receiving Jesus, or receiving

His word, may be seen as a key technical term, indicating a positive and right response to the gospel (Luke 9:48; 10:8 and 16, 38; 18:17; Acts 8:14; 11:1; 17:11). However, not all who receive the word with joy will endure. Another group, in this mixture of responses, prove to be fruitless on account of anxiety, wealth, and pleasure-seeking in this world. The last group in the parable represent the seed that falls on good ground. Luke's record of Jesus' parable provides more detail than the Gospels of Mark or Matthew. Luke alone includes the phrase 'hold it fast in an honest and good heart, and bear fruit with patience.' This suggests a specific emphasis, on Luke's part, on integrity and endurance: simply hearing is not enough; hearing needs to be honest, with the patient bearing of fruit being the result.

8:16-18 THE PARABLE OF THE LAMP – 'TAKE CARE THEN HOW YOU HEAR...'

This parable expands on what it means to 'hear' rightly. The purpose of a lamp, when placed high, is to shed light. The lamp should not be hidden (v. 16). The 'For' of verse 17 connects with the previous verse. Nothing will remain hidden forever, and everything will ultimately be known as it comes to light (see 12:2-3). Like the lamp that is put on a stand, the truth that Jesus is proclaiming, 'the good news of the kingdom of God' (8:1), is to be declared far and wide because, ultimately, His truth will become evident to all. Thus, in verse 18, Jesus' disciples who have 'ears to hear' (v. 8), and who, 'hearing the word, hold it fast ... and bear fruit with patience' (v. 15), will be given yet more insight into the truth so that they bear yet more fruit. It is God's desire that the truth He declared in Jesus should be put on a stand so that as many as possible may see it. To that end He will take from those who refuse to hear and give to those who take care how they hear (v. 18). Taking care 'how you hear' has to do with acting upon what has been heard and bearing the fruit of repentance, faith and a willingness to proclaim the gospel.

8:19-21 JESUS' CLOSE FAMILY – 'ARE THOSE WHO HEAR THE WORD OF GOD AND DO IT.'

The approach of Jesus' mother and brothers, His blood relatives (v. 19), provides Jesus with the opportunity to instruct His listeners about who it is that is closest to Him and His Kingdom. Hearing God's word and acting upon it brings a person into the family of Jesus. The two parables in verses 9-18, have spelled out what it means to 'hear the word of God and do it.' Those who hear the word and do it will be those who 'hold[s] it fast in an honest and good heart, and bear fruit with patience.' Those who hear His word and do it will publicly declare what has been made known, and thus be given access to yet more truth from God. It transpires that the group mentioned in 8:1-3 are more intimately connected to Jesus and His Kingdom than His own immediate family.

## KEY THEMES

Responding rightly to the great salvation that Jesus has come to bring means:

+ hearing His word

+ holding fast to His word with integrity

+ bearing the fruit of repentance and faith

+ joining with Him in making known what He has declared

+ receiving more truth from Him

+ being intimately connected to Him as part of His family

A wrong response to the great salvation He has come to bring is:

+ not accepting His word deep in the heart

+ not continuing to believe in times of testing

+ being distracted by anxiety, wealth, and pleasure

+ not making use of what has been revealed

Disciples should expect to see all of the above as Jesus' Kingdom is proclaimed.

## APPLICATION

*To them then:* The vast crowds that gathered to hear Jesus and witness His work are a major feature of Luke's Gospel. But numbers can be deceptive, because no one knows what is really going on in a listener's heart. Jesus was challenging His listeners and, at the same time, enabling His disciples, to make sense of what was going on in His ministry. What mattered most was an obedient response to His word. Like Isaiah before Him, Jesus' teaching was performing a dual function: bringing salvation, but also bringing judgment to those who did not have 'ears to hear'. Simply 'hearing', or being there to witness the miracles, were not adequate responses to Jesus' proclamation of the Kingdom. To be a true disciple meant responding to the challenge, in verse 15, to be the 'good soil'. Those who responded rightly to the great salvation that Jesus had come to bring would be those who kept the 'seed' of the word – it had not been snatched from them. They would continue to believe, even in times of testing (see 6:22-23). They would not be distracted from acting upon Jesus' teaching by the worries of everyday life, the pursuit of wealth, or distracting entertainment.

The right response to Jesus' word is summed up in verse 15: to 'hold it fast in an honest and good heart' is to treasure it, ponder it, embrace it, and act upon it. Mary had done this (1:38, 45); Zechariah had not (1:20). Jesus had urged the crowd to do this (6:46-49) and had warned those who did not (6:43-45). Those who did respond to His word in this way would not only 'believe and be saved' (v. 12), but also bear fruit. Their fruit-bearing faith would result in two blessings – more revelation from God (8:16-18) and deep intimacy with Jesus as family members in His Kingdom (8:19-21).

*To us now:* These verses perform the vital function of setting out what a right response to Jesus' great salvation looks like. Already Jesus has exposed the motives behind the wrong response of the Pharisees (7:29-35). This was epitomised in Simon the Pharisee. These verses reiterate the teaching of 6:49 and 1:38, 42. Simply being in a place where God's word is taught, or experiencing great spiritual 'highs', or being close to others who know God, are not enough to make one a member of God's family. What Jesus seeks is persistent attention to His word, and careful, attentive obedience. The person who responds in this manner is the person who is saved (v. 12). The sinful woman (and Mary, Peter and Levi before her) epitomise such a person. It is possible, therefore, to have been part of the vast crowd who are attracted to Jesus by His words and works, and yet never to have been saved by Him.

We must be warned by the three types of soil described in verses 12-14. For many, Satan will snatch the seed from their hearts. Others will appear to have received the word of salvation with joy, but the trials, of which Jesus spoke in 6:22-23, will show them not to have been good soil. Yet others will never bear genuine fruit, due to personal worries about children, mortgage payments, health, salary, education, achievement and the like. The desire for wealth, career advancement, or enhanced reputation in the world, will divert others. Still more will become fruitless disciples because of the distractions of entertainment, or endless holidays in retirement, or 'experiences of a lifetime'. What is sought is a response of integrity in the heart to the word of Jesus. Such a response will be rewarded with yet more revelation of the truth, for God is committed to making His truth known, and He will entrust more and more truth to those who use it responsibly. In these matters Jesus will take from the poor and give to the rich. Those who hear the words of Jesus rightly will be blessed not only with more revelation, but also with the most intimate relationship possible with Jesus. They will be family members in His Kingdom – royalty.

The key to salvation is hearing the word of Jesus.

## The Aim

The aim of this study is that we should hear the word of Jesus and be saved.

## Suggested Initial Questions

&#x8734; Introduction

&#x2198; What did we learn about salvation from Jesus' encounter with the sinful woman in the house of Simon the Pharisee? (7:36-50)

&#x8734; 8:1-3

&#x2198; What do these verses tell us about Jesus' agenda, and about His followers?

✢ 8:4-15

↘ Jesus speaks to His disciples and quotes from Isaiah 6:8-10. How does this help explain why Jesus spoke in parables?

↘ The seed in the parable of the sower represents the word of God. What prevents God's word from bearing fruit today? What do we need to do to ensure that God's word bears fruit in us?

↘ What is preventing this?

↘ How does Jesus' explanation help us understand what He means when He says, 'He who has ears to hear, let him hear.'?

✢ 8:16-18

↘ How does verse 17 encourage us to act on verse 16?

↘ How does verse 18 encourage us to act on verse 8?

↘ How does this parable build on the previous parable?

✢ 8:19-21

↘ How do verses 19-21 encourage us to implement the main message of the parables we have been studying?

✢ Summary

↘ The passage begins (verses 1-3) with a list of some of Jesus' followers. What have we learned from this study about those who follow Jesus? How will we act upon it?

# How great a Salvation! – disorder, the devil, disease, death
## Luke 8:22-56

## THE CONTEXT

Luke's aim in this section has been to show that, with the arrival of Jesus, the Saviour, the Age of God's Great Salvation has come. The section begins with two miracles of salvation: Jesus has power to save from disease and from death (7:1-17). Then, in 7:18-35, Luke shows how people responded to the evidence that Jesus is the Saviour promised by God. When people rejected Jesus they did so not because of a lack of evidence but because they refused to repent. The third part of chapter 7, verses 36-50, is at the centre of the section; it spells out what is the essence, the meaning, of salvation. Salvation from Jesus comes by grace, through faith in Christ. It comes through the forgiveness of sins (7:48-50). In the next few paragraphs, 8:1-21, Luke returns to the theme of people's response to Jesus and His great Salvation. Salvation comes through hearing the word of the Saviour and acting upon it. Those who respond in this way become Jesus' mother and brothers – part of the intimate family. However, the word of the Saviour will not take root in the hearts of all who hear it. The 'seed' that is Jesus' word does fall on good soil, but it also falls on hard, rocky or thorny ground, and does not grow. His listeners must therefore take care how they hear.

In the final part of this section Luke records two more miracles of salvation (8:22-39), and then concludes it with a further pair of miracles which have to do with faith and salvation (8:40-56).

## THE STRUCTURE

8:22-25    Salvation from this disordered creation – how great a salvation!

8:26-9    Salvation from the devil – how great a salvation!

8:40-56    Salvation from disease and death – 'Your faith has made you well [saved you]; go in peace.'

## OLD TESTAMENT NOTES

*The wind and the waves:* God's curse on creation came as a result of Adam and Eve's rebellion. The Fall meant that God's once perfect universe was now plagued not only by disease and death, but also by disorder (Gen. 3:17-19). Part of the long-promised salvation from God was to be the redemption of this disordered universe – a New Creation (Isa. 65:17; see also Romans 8:20-21).

*Death, resurrection and judgment:* In the Old Testament God had promised that His Saviour would overthrow death. Isaiah speaks of this: 'He will swallow up death for ever' (Isa. 25:7-8, cf. 26:19). This great day of resurrection was to be the day not only of salvation, but also of judgment (Dan. 12:2-3).

## TEXT NOTES

### 8:22-25 SALVATION FROM THIS DISORDERED UNIVERSE – HOW GREAT A SALVATION!

In chapter 7:21-23, Jesus gave His disciples and the disciples of John the Baptist a kind of 'grid' for making sense of His miracles. The miracles He has just performed are miracles of salvation, designed to show that He, Jesus, has arrived as the long-promised Saviour sent from God. He has come in fulfilment of God's promises, and the Baptist is His forerunner (Mal. 3:1).

Jesus' calming of the storm is far more than a demonstration of His authority over God's created order. It is proof of His identity as the Saviour who has come to usher in the Age of God's Great

Salvation from this disordered creation. On the Sea of Galilee, 13 miles long and 8 miles wide, windstorms of the kind recorded here are common. The disciples were experienced men of the Sea, but their panic indicates the severity of the situation. That Jesus could sleep in such conditions speaks not only of His calm assurance, but also of His exhaustion following a punishing preaching schedule. His sovereign assurance in the face of the storm is matched by His sovereign authority over it. The complete calm of the sea, after the raging of the waves, demonstrates that Jesus has brought about something far more than a change in the weather; stormy waves can take days to subside. Jesus' rebuke to His disciples indicates that He expects them to have already grasped the answer to the question they ask in verse 25. He is the divine Saviour, with all the authority of the Creator to redeem His disordered creation. The Age of God's Great Salvation has begun.

### 8:26-39 SALVATION FROM THE DEVIL – HOW GREAT A SALVATION!

Jesus' salvation of the demon-possessed man demonstrates His power to rescue from the greatest enemy of all – the devil. The incident is recorded by Matthew and Mark as well as Luke, but Luke alone describes the man as being 'saved' ('healed' in verse 36 is the same word as 'saved' – see the note on 7:3 in Study 12). The man's condition is detailed by Luke, the doctor: he was damaged, deranged, dangerous and dehumanised. His nakedness (he wore no clothes, v. 27) and uncleanness (he lived among the tombs, v. 27), together with his isolation (he was driven by the demon into the desert, v. 29) and violence (he would break the bonds, v. 29), all illustrate and emphasise the destructive power of evil. Like the demon-possessed man in Luke 4:33-35, this man immediately identified Jesus correctly (v. 28) – 'Jesus, Son of the Most High God'. The unclean spirit in the man acknowledged Jesus' absolute power over him, and also recognised his ultimate end – 'I beg you, do not torment me.' (v. 28) The repetition of the word 'beg' in verses 29-33 gives further evidence of Jesus' sovereignty over evil. Jesus did not 'command them [the many demons] to depart into the abyss' (v. 31), thereby indicating that God's time for the final judgment and punishment of Satan had not yet come. However, since 'he gave them [the demons] permission' to enter the pigs (v. 32), He demonstrated His absolute authority as Saviour to rescue humanity from the evil one. The Age of God's Great Salvation has arrived!

The destruction of the pigs is yet another indication of the work of the devil. The fact that Jesus allows this does not suggest a callous disregard for animal welfare. Rather, Jesus sets a priority on the salvation of humanity. The condition of the restored man, in verse 35, contrasts absolutely with his demon-possessed state. He is now calm, dressed, sane, and submissive to Jesus his teacher. To 'sit at the feet' of a teacher (v. 35) was a common expression meaning discipleship (see 10:39). The man 'begged that he might be with [Jesus]' (v. 38), in contrast to verses 28 and 31 when he had begged Jesus to leave him alone. The people's 'great fear' (vv. 35 and 37) shows their acknowledgment of Jesus' authority. They appear, however, to prefer the *status quo*, undisturbed by Jesus' liberating power (v. 37), so they ask Jesus to leave. The salvation of the man is obvious to all; once a rebel, he is now an evangelist (v. 39).

8:40-56 SALVATION FROM DISEASE AND DEATH: 'YOUR FAITH HAS MADE YOU WELL [SAVED YOU]; GO IN PEACE'

This section of Luke's Gospel, chapters 7 and 8, is brought to a conclusion with two salvation miracles. The account of the healing of Jairus' daughter – the phrase 'she will be well', in verse 50, means, literally, 'she will be saved' – is interrupted by the incident of the woman with bleeding. After twelve years of misery, she is suddenly healed. Jesus' response to the woman, 'Daughter, your faith has made you well [saved you]; go in peace', contains the key point of the whole section. It is an exact repetition of His words in chapter 7:50.

*vv40-42:* The scene described in these verses is loaded with pathos. Just as the demon-possessed man had begged Jesus (vv. 28, 31 and 38), now Jairus prostrates himself before the Lord and pleads for the life of his daughter. The interruption caused by the woman in the crowd need not have been described by Luke at this point, but deliberately he does interrupt his narrative, in order to focus his readers' attention on a second salvation incident. For the reader, tension builds. But Luke's prime concern is to highlight Jesus' words to the woman with bleeding, placing them at the structural heart of this section's conclusion.

*vv43-48:* The woman's condition (v. 43) would have rendered her unclean. Typically, Luke provides a medical note. Her faith, evidenced in verse 44, might almost be described as superstitious – it was certainly unformed and private. Jesus, from whom nothing is hidden, was unwilling to allow it to remain so. Like Peter (5:8) and Jairus (8:41) before her, the woman fell at Jesus' feet and confessed her faith publicly. Jesus' words to the woman are an exact repetition of His assurance to the sinful woman in chapter 7. The account of this woman's salvation – and the verb used in 7:50 can only mean 'save' – lies at the structural heart of chapters 7 and 8. Now, the woman with bleeding, her story placed at the heart of these concluding verses, receives the same assurance. Luke is emphasising what was taught in 7:50: salvation comes by grace, through faith in Christ. Jesus Christ has come to bring the peace of which the angels spoke (2:14). It is obtained through faith.

*vv49-56:* The delay caused by Jesus' interaction with the woman means that Jairus' daughter has now died. Jesus' words to the father, in verse 50, further emphasise the thrust of these two chapters. Once again, the phrase 'she will be well' translates the verb 'to save'; Jesus is saying to him, 'Do not fear; only believe, and she will be saved.' The resurrection of Jairus' twelve-year-old daughter sheds further light on the great salvation that Jesus has come to bring. The Old Testament had promised one who would save from death (see Old Testament Notes). This salvation miracle, like those in 7:1-17 and 8:22-39, is designed to demonstrate that Jesus, the Saviour, has come to bring the Age of God's Great Salvation. The weeping (v. 52) and the laughter (v. 53) indicate that the girl is certainly dead. To Jesus, however, death is as sleep. He is the long-promised Saviour who will one day raise the living and the dead (Isa. 26:19). To Jesus, those who are in the graves are merely asleep. The extent of the miracle is emphasised by the immediate return of the girl's appetite (v. 55).

## KEY THEMES

How Great a Salvation!

+ Jesus has arrived to save from this disordered creation

+ Jesus has arrived to save from the devil

+ Jesus has arrived to save from disease

+ Jesus has arrived to save from death

Salvation comes by grace through faith in Christ.

## APPLICATION

*To them then:* A first-century Jewish audience would have been acutely aware of God's promise, that one day He would step into His creation as Saviour and reverse the effects of God's judgment on this fallen world (see Old Testament Notes for Studies 1 to 5). Though a direct connection should never automatically be made between individual sin and individual suffering (see Luke 13:1-5), nonetheless, disease, the disorder of this creation (what we call 'natural disasters'), the devil and, ultimately, death, are all marks of God's judgment on humanity's sin. Each of the incidents in this study demonstrates that Jesus has arrived as the long-awaited Saviour. The question in 8:25 ('Who then is this ...?') is being answered even as it is asked. Throughout these verses (and the whole of chapters 7 and 8) Jesus presents Himself as the one who saves. He saves from the disordered creation, from the devil, from disease, and from death. The word 'healed' is the word 'to save' (see Text Notes). Jesus' words to the woman with bleeding are an exact repetition of His words to the sinful woman (compare 7:50 and 8:48). This confirms that Luke wants his reader to understand these 'healings' as proof of Jesus' 'salvation'.

However, Jesus' saving work continues to produce mixed responses and even to divide people. Initial fear (vv. 25, 35, 37, 47 and 50) leads some, like the local people, to reject Jesus. The response that Jesus seeks, however, is faith. Those who do believe will experience all the blessings of the benefits of the salvation that Jesus has come to bring. This salvation comes by grace, through faith in Christ. Even when this faith is embryonic (as in the case of the woman with bleeding), Jesus meets it and nourishes it.

*To us now*: whatever our material condition, the major impact of God's judgment on this fallen world is, ultimately, felt by every person born into it. No-one is immune from what we call 'natural' disasters, nor from disease, the devil's influence, or death itself. Jesus has come to save from all of these – this is how great and far-reaching His salvation is. The salvation miracles are snapshots, and also proof, of the ultimate salvation that Jesus will bring when He ushers in His New Creation. They indicate that this new age has begun.

Insofar as we fail to grasp the magnificence of the salvation that Jesus has come to bring, so far will we present an inadequate, or even a domesticated, image of Jesus. Jesus has come to do far more than improve minor unsatisfactory aspects of my life now. He has not come simply as a 'life-coach' to make small adjustments. Nor has He come primarily with a focus on transforming society here and now, or to make us better at business, personal relationships, or 'doing life'. Rather, Jesus has come with all God's authority as the Saviour who will rescue us from God's judgment on this fallen world. He saves, ultimately, from all the effects of God's judgment.

As we receive His salvation by grace, through faith, we receive as Saviour the one who will one day banish all death, all disease, all hurricanes, earthquakes, floods and famines. Satan himself will be overthrown by Jesus, and those who trust Jesus will be freed from the devil's power forever. How Great a Salvation! How Great a Saviour!

## THE AIM

The aim of this study is that we should see how great is the salvation that Jesus has come to bring.

## SUGGESTED INITIAL QUESTIONS

✤ Introduction

  ↘ What did we learn in our last study about a right response to Jesus?

✤ 8:22-25

  ↘ Read 7:22-23. What was the purpose of Jesus' miracles?

  ↘ How does Jesus calming the storm make the point about who He is and why He has come?

  ↘ Read Psalm 33:6-7. How does this add weight to the point?

  ↘ Why does Jesus rebuke His disciples in verse 25?

✤ 8:26-39

  ↘ What do we learn from Luke's description of the man with demons (vv. 26-29)?

  ↘ What do we learn about Jesus from verses 30-35?

  ↘ What do we learn from the response of the local people and the response of the man (vv. 36-39)?

✤ 8:40-56

  ↘ What do we learn about Jairus' daughter and the woman with bleeding (vv. 40-43)?

  ↘ How would you describe the woman's faith (v. 44)?

  ↘ Look up 7:50. How does this compare with 8:48 and 8:50?

  ↘ How does Luke's description of the scene at Jairus' house help to show that Jairus' daughter was definitely dead?

  ↘ What does Jesus healing the woman and raising Jairus' daughter prove?

✤ Summary

  ↘ This passage brings to a close the section that began in 7:1. How has our study of this section increased your confidence in the content of the gospel?

  ↘ How has our study of this section increased your confidence in the credibility of the gospel?

  ↘ How has our study of this section increased your readiness to communicate the gospel to others?

# PART ONE (D)

## LUKE 9:1-50

# *THE SAVIOUR'S SUMMONS*

# Section Notes
## Part One (D): 9:1-50
## The Saviour's Summons

Luke 9:1-50 forms the central block of teaching in Luke's Gospel. This 'bridge' section brings to a conclusion the first half of the Gospel and prepares the way for the main emphasis of the second. It contains numerous references to the Exodus, and these references help to describe more precisely the identity of Jesus and His mission, in terms of a fulfilment of the Old Testament rescue of Israel at the Exodus (see Old Testament Notes for Study 16). Jesus has come to accomplish everything that the Exodus anticipated. There are three main themes in verses 1-50.

### IDENTITY AND MISSION
The issue of Jesus' identity has been on the agenda for several chapters (7:18-20). In 9:1-50, His identity is confirmed first by Jesus Himself, as He feeds the five thousand and enables the disciples to see who He is (v. 20 'the Christ of God'), then by the Law and the Prophets, represented by Moses and Elijah appearing at the Transfiguration of Jesus (v. 30), and then by God Himself, speaking at the Transfiguration (v. 35 'This is my Son, my Chosen One'). Hand in hand with this recognition of Jesus comes a focus on His mission, or purpose. As with the matter of identity, the nature of His mission is confirmed by Jesus Himself (v. 22 'The Son of Man must suffer many things'), and then by Moses and Elijah (v. 31). Thus the identity of Christ is made clear in the first half

of the section by God the Son, and in the second half by God the Father; then, the mission of Christ is made clear in the first half of the section by Jesus' words and in the second half by the Father's word (the Law and the Prophets).

## DISCIPLESHIP AND SERVICE

The section begins and ends with the theme of service. The disciples are commissioned to proclaim the gospel (vv. 1-6), but they are unable to feed the crowd (v. 13) or heal the boy (v. 40), and they fail spectacularly in the realm of humble service (vv. 46-50). Right at the heart of this section, sandwiched between the two blocks of material on Jesus' identity and mission (vv. 18-22 and 28-36) is Jesus' summons to discipleship. It seems that the disciples will not be able to follow, or serve, until they have had their eyes opened to the redemptive work that Jesus has come to do.

## REVELATION:

The final theme in these verses is that of understanding. In the first half of the section Herod, the human king of Israel, is unable to see who Jesus is (vv. 7-9). Peter, in verse 20, grasps who Jesus is, but only after Jesus' revelation of His supernatural power through the feeding of the five thousand. In the second half of the section the disciples show themselves to be part of the 'faithless and twisted generation' (v. 41); they are kept from understanding the mission of Jesus (v. 45). Thus, in the first half of the section (vv. 1-27), Peter and the disciples have understood Jesus' *identity*, but in the second half of the section they have clearly failed to understand His *mission*, and what it might look like to serve Him. Only following Jesus' resurrection does it become clear that the Son of Man must suffer and, on the third day, rise. Even then, sight is given only as the risen Jesus enables it, and sight comes through understanding the Law and the Prophets. There are tight connections between Jesus blessing the bread and the fish at the feeding of the five thousand, and Jesus blessing the bread and feeding His disciples at the house in Emmaus (24:30). Here, in chapter 9, Jesus' disciples are enabled to see who He is as a result of His feeding them, just as God fed the

Israelites through Moses. Their eyes, however, remain closed to His
mission (v. 45). It is only as the risen Christ opens the eyes of His
disciples to understand the Law and the Prophets (24:25-27; 32)
that they are enabled to see Him for who He is, to understand what
He came to do, and so to serve Him as He truly desires.

## THE STRUCTURE

(the structure for the whole section is laid out below)

9:1-6      Serving the Saviour – the disciples' commission

9:7-9      Seeing the Saviour – Herod perplexed and unable to see

9:10-17    Being served by the Saviour – the feeding of the five
           thousand

9:18-22    The Saviour's identity and mission

9:23-27    The Saviour's summons

9:28-36    The Saviour's mission and identity

9:37-43    Being served by the Saviour – this 'faithless and
           twisted generation'

9:43-45    Seeing the Saviour – the disciples fail to see

9:46-50    Serving the Saviour – the disciples' failure

STUDY 16

# The Saviour's Identity and Mission
# Luke 9:1-27

## THE CONTEXT

Luke 9:1-50 brings Part One of Luke's Gospel to a conclusion. Aiming to bring certainty to his reader's mind (1:4), Luke has explained Jesus' credentials (1:5–4:13), Jesus' manifesto (4:14–6:49), and Jesus' mission (7:1–8:56). Now he begins to explain what it will look like for Jesus' disciples to follow Him.

## OLD TESTAMENT NOTES

*The Exodus:* When God redeemed Israel from slavery in Egypt, He fed them in the wilderness with manna from heaven (Exod. 16). This supernatural feeding of God's people was intended both as a demonstration of God's provision and as a test of His people's faithfulness (Exod. 16:4, Ps. 78:24-25). Israel failed the test repeatedly (Ps. 106:13-15). The people of Israel are described as 'a perverse generation, children in whom is no faithfulness.'; God declares, 'I will hide my face from them' (Deut. 32:20).

*The Christ of God:* The Messiah, the Son of David, is the Christ of God (see Old Testament Notes for Studies 1 and 6).

*The Son of Man:* God's eternal King and Judge is the Son of Man (see Old Testament Notes for Study 8).

## TEXT NOTES

### 9:1-6 SERVING THE SAVIOUR

For the first time Jesus includes the twelve Apostles in His work of gospel proclamation. The twelve were appointed in Chapter 6; now they are commissioned. Their mission mirrors their master's (4:43). Their authority over demons and disease, like His, indicates the arrival of King Jesus and the breaking in of His new Age of Salvation. Jesus' command that they take nothing for their journey (9:3) is not intended to apply to all missionary service (22:36); rather, it is an indication of the urgency of the task in hand. In verse 5, to fail to 'receive' the Apostle who proclaims the Kingdom is to reject the King (see also 10:5, 8). These verses see the Apostles being active in the service of the King.

### 9:7-9 SEEING THE SAVIOUR

Herod, the king of Israel, is alerted to the gathering momentum of Jesus' ministry. Representing the failed nation of Israel, Herod is unable to grasp who Jesus is. He is 'perplexed' and cannot see. It is clear to him that Jesus is a great one. Malachi had promised that one like Elijah will come (see Old Testament Notes for Studies 1 and 2), but in Herod's mind there is confusion and uncertainty. It appears that, like the Pharisees and the lawyers, he has not accepted the baptism of John (7:30).

### 9:10-17 BEING SERVED BY THE SAVIOUR

The feeding of the five thousand in Luke's Gospel emphasises the failure of Jesus' Apostles in His service, and also Jesus' provision as He serves the needs of the people. (It matches the subsequent failure and provision in vv. 37-43.) This miracle has close connections to the Exodus and God's miraculous feeding of His rescued people (see Old Testament Notes). Luke draws attention to the time, 'the day began to wear away'; the location, 'we are here in a desolate place'; the command, 'You give them something to eat', and the number of people, 'there were about five thousand men' (together with the women and children it must have been a vast crowd). Jesus blesses the loaves, breaks them, and gives them to His disciples to feed the crowd (v. 16). Just as with the manna in the wilderness, there is more than enough to go around. The twelve baskets gathered by the disciples are symbolic of the twelve tribes of Israel. Jesus has demonstrated Himself to be able to serve His people and provide all their needs. He does what His Apostles cannot do. Their ministry will be both enabled and empowered by Him.

### 9:18-22 THE SAVIOUR'S IDENTITY AND MISSION

In the context of Jesus' supernatural feeding of His people, Jesus now asks the disciples, 'Who do the crowds say that I am?' At first it seems that they are as perplexed as Herod – they simply recite the ideas found in verses 7-8. Peter, however, demonstrates that his disciples *have* perceived who He is. Since Peter's declaration comes after the feeding of the five thousand, it suggests that the Apostles' ability to perceive the true identity of Jesus has been enabled only by His divine provision. However, Jesus is not content that His disciples should grasp His identity, and no more. He immediately presses things further, insisting that, as the Son of Man (see Old Testament Notes), His mission is to face suffering, rejection, death and resurrection.

### 9:23-27 THE SAVIOUR'S SUMMONS

These verses lie at the structural heart of the section (see *The Structure* in the Section Notes above). Verses 24, 25 and 26 are each tightly linked by the word 'For'.

Verse 23 spells out the cost of true discipleship. To 'deny himself' is not simply to forgo little pleasures in life. The word means 'to disown', and the model for such denial is Jesus. Jesus did not go His own way, but God's. He sought not His own glory, but His Father's. He did not pursue His own agenda or good, but the agenda and good of God. To 'take up his cross' is not a picture simply of bearing a few small hardships. The cross was a first-century instrument of torture and death. The disciple therefore is to consider him or herself dead to self. The word 'anyone' at the start of the sentence suggests that this kind of cross-shaped discipleship is not an optional extra – it is for everyone. The word 'daily' suggests that it is not an occasional affair, but an everyday affair.

Verse 24 explains why genuine discipleship must be like this. The key to understanding the first half of the verse lies in the second half: Jesus commands the true disciple to 'lose his life *for my sake*'. To lose life, then, is to place life in His hands and to live wholeheartedly and unreservedly for Him…'Take my life, and let it be consecrated, Lord, to thee'.[1] To 'save his life' is, for a disciple, to cling on to his or her own agenda apart from Jesus. The close link between verses 23-24 and the earlier verses, verses 21-22, must be stressed: the Son of Man went to His death to carry God's judgment on the sin and selfish ambition of man. That which the world cherishes is that which God hates. The true disciple will understand this and thus seek, with His help, to put to death everything that God hates and for which Christ died. The key to active putting to death of sin lies in a clear grasp of the cross of Christ.

Verse 25 provides further incentive for true discipleship. The incentive that Jesus gives is in the form of the strongest possible warning. To gain the whole world but to lose oneself is an image of utter dereliction – the poor little rich man. To cling on to precious desires and sinful habits, at the cost of destruction because of being apart from Jesus, is to lose everything!

Verse 26 drives the point deeper still. The Son of Man will come in judgment 'in his glory and the glory of the Father and of the holy angels.' For the Son of Man to be ashamed of a would-be disciple on the Day of Judgment is a prospect of utter despair. What does it mean, to be ashamed of Jesus and of His words? It is to be ashamed of Jesus and of His teaching. Jesus' disciples are to stand with, by, and for the word of God in the Bible – even in the face of unpopularity and persecution.

Verse 27 provides strong and positive encouragement. Peter, John and James are about to witness the Transfiguration of Jesus, and many of His disciples would see Him rise from the dead. Thus, in spite of the costly nature of true discipleship, His disciples should take heart from the glorious Kingdom which Jesus' death and resurrection would establish.

---

1.    From the hymn by Frances Ridley Havergal.

## KEY THEMES

*The identity and mission of Jesus:* Jesus is the Christ, and the Son of Man. His Kingdom will be established as He lays down His life and rises again.

*Discipleship and service:* Jesus' disciples are to take up their cross daily and follow Him.

*Revelation:* Jesus' disciples alone perceive the true identity of Jesus; He enables them to see this.

## APPLICATION

*To them then:* Having been shown the identity of Jesus – He is 'The Christ of God.' – His disciples now need to understand His mission. The mission of Jesus, His suffering, death and resurrection, provide the model for the true disciple and for genuine service. The service for which the disciples are commissioned is only possible because Jesus enables them to see who He is. Herod, king of Israel and thus of the historic people of God, could not grasp Jesus' identity.

Faced with a huge crowd of hungry people, Jesus' disciples could not feed Jesus' people. When Jesus does for His disciples what God did for His people at the Exodus, His disciples are enabled to recognise Jesus as the Christ, and then to serve Him. Their genuine discipleship is to take the form of cross-shaped, self-denying, wholehearted, sacrificial loyalty to Jesus and to His word.

*To us now:* True discipleship involves denying self and putting self, and every sinful habit and ambition, to death. My sin is what took Jesus to the cross. God hates my sin and punished it at the cross. With my sin now dealt with, through Jesus' death on the cross, I am to take up my cross in a daily battle with sin. The image is one of death. I am to put sin to death. This is not simply for the 'super-hero' Christian. It is not an optional affair – it is for everyone. It is not an occasional affair – it is for every day. To 'save my life' is to live for me, my personal agenda, my comfort and my ambition. To 'lose life' is to lose my life for Jesus' sake. Thus, genuine discipleship means putting personal ambition and goals to death as we place Jesus and the service of

His Kingdom as our primary goal. This will impact both the small habits and the personal peccadilloes in our lives. If we know that there is something we do, or something we love, that Jesus hates, it is to be killed off! Every area of life is involved – what we watch, how we spend our time and our money, our sex life, our family life, our work life. But it also involves the big decisions – where I choose to live, what job I do and how much time I devote to it, whether I accept promotion, whether and whom I marry, and so forth. Whatever gifts and abilities I have are to be placed at His disposal, in His service, as I take up my cross daily and follow Him.

We will frequently find ourselves wanting to cling on to a life lived for myself; we will want to 'gain the whole world'. This will result in our losing everything. On other occasions we will find ourselves tempted to distance ourselves from Jesus, and also from His words – especially when His words are unpopular with the world. If we are ashamed of Jesus and His teaching in this life, He will be ashamed of us in the next. We love to speak of 'my goals', 'my ambitions', 'my career'. The true Christian is to have no career, ambition or goal other than selfless service of Christ the King. 'Career', as understood by the world, is not a Christian concept.

## THE AIM

The aim of this study is that we should see who Jesus is, and so be ready to follow Him.

## SUGGESTED INITIAL QUESTIONS

✤ Introduction
  ↘ What was Luke's aim in writing his Gospel?
  ↘ How have chapters 7 and 8 achieved his aim?
✤ 9:1-9
  ↘ What impression of Jesus' mission is given by:
    ✦ His commission of the twelve?
    ✦ the reception they receive?
    ✦ Herod's reaction?

✤ 9:10-17

  ↘ Read Psalm 78:17-27. How do these verses help us understand what God's feeding of His people at the Exodus was all about?

  ↘ How does the miracle recorded in verses 10-17 answer the Apostles' perplexity about the identity of Jesus? What does verse 13 teach us about the Apostles?

✤ 9:18-22

  ↘ What has Peter seen that Herod has failed to see?

  ↘ What does Peter still need to learn?

✤ 9:23-27

  ↘ Read verse 23 carefully. What is the connection between verse 22 and verse 23?

  ↘ How does Jesus' summons to discipleship differ from our thinking about what discipleship involves?

  ↘ To whom does verse 23 apply, and when does it apply?

  ↘ How do verses 24 and 25 explain why verse 23 must be as it is?

  ↘ In verses 26 and 27 there are two incentives to genuine discipleship. How do they work?

✤ Summary

  ↘ What have we learned in this section about the identity of Jesus, His mission, and what it means to be a true disciple?

# The Saviour's Mission and Identity Confirmed
## Luke 9:23-50

### THE CONTEXT

Chapter 9:1-50 forms the central section in Luke's Gospel. In the first half of the chapter, Jesus' disciples, with His enabling, see who He is. Jesus then explains His mission – to die and rise again – and summons them to discipleship. Both these themes, of mission and identity, are repeated in the second half of the section. Jesus' mission, as Moses and Elijah discuss with Him, is His 'departure' (Exodus) which He will accomplish at Jerusalem. His identity is that of God's Son, as the voice of God confirms.

The failure of the disciples to heal the boy with the unclean spirit shows them to be part of the 'faithless and twisted generation' of the Exodus. They need salvation. But the disciples are kept from seeing the rescue mission of Jesus, and this failure of sight leads to a failure in service. Thus, in this central section, Luke provides a 'bridge' from the first to the second half of his Gospel. The key theme of Jesus' identity has been grasped and understood. But the disciples are unable to understand what the Law and the Prophets had pointed to: a suffering, sin-bearing Son of Man, who will establish His rule and save His people through His death. God's command to 'listen' (v. 35) and Jesus' command, 'Let these words sink into your ears:' (v. 44), indicate the importance of paying close attention. However, the disciples will be unable to see, and will be kept from understanding His mission, until Jesus finally opens their eyes to understand the Scriptures, following His death and resurrection. The disciples on the road to Emmaus are described as 'foolish ones, and slow of heart to believe' (24:25); they are just like the wilderness generation. Only as the risen Jesus explains the Scriptures do they 'see'. Only then do they grasp what it means to walk in the footsteps of their master, and only then are they enabled to serve as the true people of God.

## THE STRUCTURE

(the structure for the whole section is laid out below)

| | |
|---|---|
| 9:1-6 | Serving the Saviour – the disciples commissioned |
| 9:7-9 | Seeing the Saviour – Herod perplexed and unable to see |
| 9:10-17 | Being served by the Saviour – the feeding of the five thousand |
| 9:18-22 | The Saviour's identity and mission |
| 9:23-27 | The Saviour's summons |
| 9:28-36 | The Saviour's mission and identity |
| 9:37-43 | Being served by the Saviour – this 'faithless and twisted generation' |
| 9:43-45 | Seeing the Saviour – the disciples fail to see |
| 9:46-50 | Serving the Saviour – the disciples' failure |

## OLD TESTAMENT NOTES

*The Exodus (see Old Testament Notes for Study 4)*: Jesus discusses 'his departure' with Moses and Elijah (v. 31). Literally, the Greek text has 'his Exodus'. Also, Jesus' feeding of the five thousand contains deliberate similarities to Moses' feeding of God's people at the Exodus. Similarly, Jesus' analysis of the crowd as a 'faithless and twisted generation' compares them to Israel at the Exodus (Deut. 32:20). Thus this whole section is permeated with allusions to the Exodus, as Jesus indicates that the mission, which He is to accomplish through His death, is a fulfilment of the redemption that God has anticipated for His people at the Exodus.

*Moses and Elijah*: The Law and the Prophets of the Old Testament are represented by Moses and Elijah (see Luke 24:27 and 32). The contents of the Old Testament can also be summarised by the phrase 'the Law of Moses, the Psalms and the Prophets'.

*'This is my Son, my Chosen One'*: See Old Testament Notes for Study 6.

*Blindness*: In Isaiah, God blinds His people in judgment on their sins (Isa. 6:9-10; 29:10-11; 44:18). God is described as 'a God who hides [himself]' (Isa. 45:15). The Servant figure, in Isaiah, is the one who will open the eyes of the spiritually blind and enable them to see (Isa. 42:6-7; 61:1-2).

*'The Son of Man'*: The Ruler of God's eternal Kingdom is described as 'one like a son of man'. His kingdom is everlasting and is made up of people from all nations (Dan. 7:13-14). This figure 'with a human appearance' is also witnessed in His dazzling splendour by Ezekiel (Ezek.1:26-27). Further reference to this son of man can be found in the Psalms (Ps. 80:15-17).

## TEXT NOTES

### 9:23-27 THE SAVIOUR'S SUMMONS

At the structural centre of this section lies the command of Jesus to every disciple, to 'take up his cross daily and follow me' (v. 23). Failure to heed Jesus' summons may result in immediate gratification (vv. 24 and 25). It ends in destitution (v. 25) and dereliction (v. 26). Some of those with Jesus at this time will see Him not only transfigured (vv. 28-36), but also resurrected (24:1-49). Thus, among Jesus' immediate listeners, many would live to see His Kingdom established.

### 9:28-36 THE SAVIOUR'S MISSION AND IDENTITY

Peter, John and James are given a glimpse of Jesus in His heavenly glory. This alteration of Jesus' appearance and clothing on the mountain is known as 'the transfiguration'. Jesus has just been speaking of His imminent suffering, and has referred to Himself as 'the Son of Man' (9:21). He will shortly say these things again (9:44). The dramatic sight of Jesus in glory, transfigured as He will be after His death and resurrection, gives His disciples further confirmation of His identity and His mission. Moses and Elijah, representing the Law and the Prophets (see Old Testament Notes), discuss His 'departure'. The word for 'departure' is, literally, 'Exodus'. The Exodus was the great Old Testament event when God saved His people from slavery in Egypt, by means of a sacrificial lamb that would carry God's judgment in the place of the eldest son in each Israelite family (see Old Testament Notes for Study 4). Thus the glorified Moses and Elijah appear on the mountain and confirm for Jesus' disciples what He has already told them, concerning His mission to save His people: as the sacrificial lamb He will die and rise again to life. Once again, the Old Testament Scriptures are shown to be the key to understanding the mission of Jesus.

In verses 32-36 the emphasis shifts from the mission of Jesus, as Son of Man, to His identity. Peter has recognised Jesus as 'The Christ of God.' (v. 20) God now confirms Peter's confession. The cloud (v. 34) indicates the presence and glory of God (see Exodus 19:16; 40:34). The voice from the cloud refers to Jesus as 'my Son' and 'my Chosen One', combining Old Testament references to God's anointed King and to His Suffering Servant (see Old Testament Notes for this study and also for Study 6). On only two other occasions in the Gospels is God's voice heard directly – at Jesus' baptism (3:21-22) and in John 12:28. Here, at the Transfiguration, God confirms Jesus' identity – 'my Son', and also His mission – 'my Chosen One'. Jesus is the Messiah King and also the Suffering Servant who will die to save His people. God is thus adding his immediate audible word to His written word through Moses (representing the Law) and through Elijah (representing the Prophets). There can be no denying that God is referring to Jesus – when the cloud lifted 'Jesus was found alone.'

9:37-43 BEING SERVED BY THE SAVIOUR – THIS 'FAITHLESS AND TWISTED GENERATION'

The disciples' failure with the boy who suffered seizures seems strange. Jesus had given them authority to conduct this kind of healing, as evidence of the arrival of His Kingdom (9:2-6). Their failure and the crowd's unbelief cause Jesus to cry out in exasperation. Verse 41 is a direct reference to the Exodus generation (see Old Testament Notes). Thus, all the events of this chapter point toward the saving work that Jesus came to do, in fulfilment of the promises of the Old Testament. He has come to provide true food from heaven for God's people (vv. 10-17); to 'suffer… and be killed, and on the third day be raised' (v. 22), and to accomplish His Exodus at Jerusalem (v. 31). As the Son of Man He will accomplish everything that the Exodus pointed towards. He will do this through His suffering and His sin-bearing death.

### 9:43B-45 SEEING THE SAVIOUR – THE DISCIPLES FAIL TO SEE

In verse 44 Jesus repeats some of the 'words' that had been recorded earlier in the chapter. He is wanting to drive home the point that he had made earlier (vv. 21-23). As the Son of Man He was about to be delivered over to death. The phrase 'Let these words sink into your ears:' (v. 44) is very emphatic. Jesus wants to impress on His disciples the fact that the work of redemption, of which Moses and Elijah spoke, and about which God the Father commanded His disciples to listen, really will involve His suffering, and also their cross-bearing discipleship.

However, the disciples are deliberately prevented from seeing the necessity of Jesus' death. This reminds us that God blinded His people in Isaiah's day, as part of His judgment on them (see Old Testament Notes). It shows that the judgment of God on His people is not lifted until Jesus brings the salvation that God has promised (see Old Testament Notes). The same theme of 'blinding' is repeated in Luke 18:34 and in 24:16. It is only as the risen Lord Jesus 'interpreted to them in all the Scriptures the things concerning himself' (24:27) that their eyes were opened to see Him. It will require the death and resurrection of Christ for the people of a 'faithless and twisted generation' to be saved. They will only understand His death and resurrection through the Old Testament Law and the Prophets. For now, the disciples are kept in ignorance of the mission to which the Law and the Prophets, and God Himself, have testified.

9:46-50 Serving the Saviour – the disciples' failure

The disciples' failure to see the essence of the character of God (selfless service) gives rise to the failure of verse 46. This characteristic human trait is found again in the disciples at the Passover meal (22:24-27). They are unable to see that the Son of Man is 'among you as the one who serves.' (22:27) By way of illustration Jesus brings a child to His side. The child in the first century had no status or rank and could offer no reward or return for service. Furthermore, in the second half of the Gospel the child becomes symbolic of any disciple who humbly receives Jesus' rule and forgiveness (18:16-17). Thus, genuine discipleship for redeemed members of the people of God involves not only the daily taking up of the cross, but also humble service, walking in the footsteps of the Son of Man who was delivered into the hands of men for the sake of His people. In God's Kingdom, selflessness in the service of Jesus is rewarded.

This selfless service will be exhibited by a recognition and a welcome extended towards all who claim genuine allegiance to Jesus (vv. 49-50), even if a person's allegiance does not involve much understanding.

## Key Themes

*Jesus' mission:* He has come, in accordance with the Scriptures, to fulfil everything that the Exodus anticipated.

*Jesus' identity:* He is the Son of Man, the Son of God, the Chosen One.

*Blindness/faithlessness:* Those belonging to a faithless and twisted generation are kept from seeing Jesus. Sight comes, by miraculous intervention, from the Scriptures as they are explained.

*Failure to serve:* True discipleship is never possible without spiritual sight and understanding. Genuine discipleship means humble service in the footsteps of the master.

## Application

*To them then:* The purpose of the second half of this central section of Luke's Gospel is to drive home the necessity of Jesus' death. It is through His death that Jesus will lift God's judgment and establish

His royal Kingdom as the Son of Man. The need for Jesus' death is demonstrated by the spiritual dullness of this 'faithless and twisted generation'. Like the Israelites of old, even the disciples are powerless to save, they are hopeless in service, and they remain blinded by God to His work. Thus the disciples' failure in verses 37-48 encapsulates the great problem of humanity. Blind, impotent, unbelieving and 'twisted', the need for the rescue of which the Law and the Prophets speak is absolute.

*To us now*: These verses should strengthen our confidence in both the credibility and the content of the gospel. In the first half of this central section we were challenged to deny self, to take up our cross and to follow Jesus. We were warned of the dangers of not doing so. With Jesus' identity and mission re-asserted at the Transfiguration, we have greater incentive for true discipleship. Why should we deny self, take up our cross and follow Jesus? Because He really is God's King and He has come to accomplish God's rescue of humanity! Not only so, but with the weakness and 'perversity' of the human heart exposed, and with the inability of humanity (because of blindness) to perceive the truth that comes from God, we are shown that we desperately need the rescue Jesus has come to bring. Just as we cannot follow Jesus in the way He desires without first being rescued by Him, neither can we serve Him rightly without first being rescued by Him at the cross. We are, by nature, blind and we need to be given sight. We are faithless and perverse and we need salvation. We are self-serving and vainly ambitious, and we need Jesus to humble us and teach us. Moses and Elijah know this (it is what the Law and the Prophets spoke of), and God the Father confirms it.

Jesus, through His death on the cross, is about to show us that He is 'among [us] as the one who serves.' (22:27) This will form the 'agenda' for the second half of Luke's Gospel, where we will see that Jesus has come as the royal saviour who serves His people by dying on the cross. Once we grasp this truth, it will impact every aspect of every part of our lives, and we will give ourselves in the service of Jesus: 'For he who is least among all of you is the one who is great.'(9:48) We will not be able to grasp this without the risen Jesus opening our eyes to see it. We will only grasp this as we are taught by Him from the Old Testament Scriptures.

## The Aim

The aim of this study is that we should grasp the centrality of Jesus' death and resurrection to all genuine and useful discipleship.

## Suggested Initial Questions

℞ Introduction

↘ What did we learn about Jesus' identity and mission in 9:1-27?

↘ What did we learn about discipleship?

℞ 9:28-36

↘ Moses and Elijah represent the Old Testament Law and the Prophets. How does the conversation in verses 28-33 help us understand what is going on?

↘ How does this help make sense of what Jesus said in verses 21-22?

↘ How do verses 34-36 add weight to what the disciples have learned (v. 20), what Jesus has said (vv. 21-22) and what Jesus desires (vv. 23-27)?

℞ 9:37-43

↘ Look up Deuteronomy 32:20. How does this help us understand what Jesus means in verse 41?

↘ What does this incident suggest about the disciples?

℞ 9:43-50

↘ What is it that the disciples are unable to grasp?

↘ How does their failure show up in their squabbling?

↘ How does their failure show up in verses 49-50?

↘ In what ways do we also fail in these areas? Why?

℞ Summary

↘ What will be needed if the disciples are to understand and practise *true* discipleship? (The answer is to be found in verses 21-22, 30-36, and 44-45)

# Group Preparation Questions

## Luke 1:1-38

✤ Please spend part of your time in prayer for your group and reading through Luke 1:1-38 several times. For the remainder of your time:

✤ Read Luke 1:1-4 and Luke 24:44-49. What does Luke reveal in these 'bookends' about the purpose of his book? Spend some time praying that this purpose would be achieved as we study Luke together.

✤ What are the clues in the text of Luke 1:1-38 that Luke intends us to compare Zechariah and Mary? How do Zechariah and Mary differ?

✤ If you have time: Read Malachi 3:1-5 and 4:1-6. How does this help us to understand the references to Elijah in Luke 1?

# Luke 1:39-80

✻ Salvation is an important theme in this chapter. In what different ways does Luke give it prominence?

✻ Read 1 Samuel 2. What similarities can you find between Hannah's prayer and Mary's song?

STUDY 3

# Luke 2:1-21

✤ Luke told us in his introduction that his Gospel will give us grounds for 'certainty concerning the things you have been taught' (1:4), and that he would achieve this both by showing us what the eyewitnesses say, and by showing us how this fulfils Old Testament prophecy.

✤ Eyewitness: What details of 2:1-31 bear the hallmarks of eyewitness testimony?

✤ Fulfilment: What Old Testament character is mentioned repeatedly and why?

STUDY 4

# Luke 2:22-52

✤ Think about the structure of the passage and then divide the chapter into 2 sections:

    ↘    How does Luke mark the sections?

    ↘    How do they fit together?

✤ What more do we learn about Jesus' mission in section 1?

✤ What more do we learn about Jesus' identity in section 2?

STUDY 5

# Luke 3:1-20

✤ What is John the Baptist's message?

✤ How does this message relate to salvation and the forgiveness of sins?

# Luke 3:21-4:13

✤ This passage is rich with Old Testament background. It will be useful for the study if in your preparation you familiarise yourself with some of the Old Testament quotations and allusions:

✤ Who is described as God's son in these verses: Exodus 4:22, Hosea 11:1, 2 Samuel 7:12-14, Psalm 2?

✤ Jesus quotes the Old Testament directly to the devil. Read Deuteronomy 6:4-17 and 8:1-10. What is the historical context of these passages? What parallels do they have with Jesus and His situation?

STUDY 7

# Luke 4:14-44

✤ For this week's prep we're going to look in a bit more detail at the Isaiah passage that Jesus reads from in the synagogue in Luke 4:17-21.

✤ In Isaiah's context, the poor and the captives are in this state because of the Babylonian exile. How does this affect the way that we read these verses?

✤ Blindness also has a particular meaning in Isaiah. Read Isaiah 6:8-13 and Isaiah 29:1-12, and consider how this affects the way we read Luke 4:17-21.

✤ What is striking about where Jesus ends the quotation (see Isaiah 61:1-2)?

# Luke 5:1-32

✤ The passage divides neatly into four separate incidents.

✤ What do the four incidents have in common with each other?

✤ How does each incident relate to the passage before it and after it?

✤ How do these incidents serve to clarify for us why Jesus came?

# Luke 5:33-6:11

℘ What do each of the sections have in common? (Include in your prep the previous two scenes in 5:17-32)

℘ What progression is there through the scenes?

# Luke 6:12-36

✤ We've seen repeatedly in Luke that we can only understand individual episodes by relating them to what happens before and after.

✤ Read verses 12-16. How does this relate to last week's passage? Why is this a fitting time for Jesus to appoint His apostles?

✤ What connections can you find between verses 20-26 and verses 27-36? How does understanding verses 20-26 make possible the extraordinary ethic outlined in verses 27-36?

# Luke 6:37-49

✤ Divide the passage into three or four sections, and give each section a title (this is a helpful step when studying any passage in the Bible).

✤ Can you identify any flow of thought between the sections? (This is harder.)

# Luke 7:1-35

🖎 Because of its repetition, we notice that Luke gives prominence to John's question in verses 19-20. Why? How does it provide a lens through which we can read the rest of the passage?

🖎 Put this passage in context by revising some of the back story in chapters 1–6. In particular try to identify passages that help our understanding of 7:18-20 and 7:29-30.

# Luke 7:36-50

✤ How are Simon and the woman contrasted in verses 36-39?

✤ How does Jesus explain the difference between them in the rest of the passage?

✤ At first sight, verse 47 seems to say that the woman is forgiven because of her love for Jesus. What reasons can you find in the passage why this cannot be Jesus' meaning?

# Luke 8:1-21

✤ As we've seen before, one of the main clues to the author's purpose is the way he gathers together episodes that make a similar point.

✤ Can you identify the idea that verses 1-8, verses 9-15, verses 16-18 and verses 19-21 have in common?

✤ Can you identify equivalents in your own life of the various dangers Jesus points to?

# Luke 8:22-56

✥ Read Luke 8:22-56. Jesus brings salvation in four life-threatening situations. Looking at each in turn, consider how Luke describes:

↘ mankind's helplessness before Jesus' intervention

↘ the comprehensive solution Jesus brings

↘ people's reactions to what Jesus has done

# Luke 9:1-27

✣ You will notice that Luke draws a contrast between the responses of Herod (vv. 7-9) and Peter (vv. 18-20), using similar language each time. What clues does he give about WHY they respond differently? How does the context help (e.g. 3:1-20)? What is the significance of the intervening verses, verses 10-17?

✣ What connections can you find between Jesus' fate in verses 21-22, and what He asks of would-be disciples in verses 23-27? How does this challenge us in our own Christian walk?

# Luke 9:28-50

✤ In the last study we saw that Jesus was the Christ who must suffer.

✤ In this passage, in what various ways does Luke seek to strengthen these convictions about Jesus' identity and mission?

✤ What indications are there that the disciples have not entirely grasped this?

# Bibliography

## Technical Commentaries

Darrell L. Bock, *Baker Exegetical Commentary on the New Testament, Luke* (Baker Academic: Grand Rapids, Michigan, 2006)

John Nolland, *Word Biblical Commentary 35 Luke* (Thomas Nelson: Nashville, TN, 1989)

## Popular Commentaries

David Gooding, *According to Luke* (InterVarsity Press: Leicester, England, 1987)

Leon Morris, *The Gospel According to St Luke Tyndale New Testament Commentaries* (InterVarsity Press: Leicester, England, 1974)

John G. Mason, *Luke, Reading the Bible Today Series* (Aquila Press: Sydney, Australia, 2012)

READ / MARK / LEARN

# JOHN

"Read / Mark / Learn *has taught hundreds of us over the years
to know our Bibles and our God better."*
—Hugh Palmer

## St HELEN'S
BISHOPSGATE

ISBN 978-1-84550-361-1

# Read Mark Learn: John

## *A Small Group Bible Study*

### St. Helen's Bishopsgate

"This series of books is superb for personal study, and for helping those who teach the Bible to others. I've been getting a lot to give away to others now. The level is accessible, the reasoning clear, the application careful. Faithful and concise, never missing the big picture. Excellent."

Mark Dever
Senior Pastor, Capitol Hill Baptist Church
President, 9Marks.org, Washington, DC

"Read / Mark / Learn has taught thousands of us over the years to know our Bibles and our God better."

Hugh Palmer
Rector, All Souls Langham Place, London

"These study notes take us to the heart of the meaning of the Gospel."

John Chapman

"The art of simplification is not an easy one, but here it is at its best, and put to excellent use."

D. A. Carson
Research Professor of New Testament, Trinity Evangelical
Divinity School, Deerfield, Illinois

READ / MARK / LEARN

ROMANS

"The art of simplification is not an easy one,
but here it is at its best."
--Don Carson

ST HELEN'S
BISHOPSGATE

ISBN 978-1-84550-362-8

# Read Mark Learn: Romans
## *A Small Group Bible Study*
### St. Helen's Bishopsgate

This series of books is superb for personal study, and for helping those who teach the Bible to others. I've been getting a lot to give away to others now. The level is accessible, the reasoning clear, the application careful. Faithful and concise, never missing the big picture. Excellent.

Mark Dever
Senior Pastor, Capitol Hill Baptist Church
President, 9Marks.org, Washington, DC

Read / Mark / Learn has taught thousands of us over the years to know our Bibles and our God better.

Hugh Palmer
Rector, All Souls Langham Place, London

Supremely beneficial for clarifying the message of Romans, providing quality training for Bible study leaders and planting deep missionary convictions in young Christians.

Richard Coekin
Senior Minister, CO-MISSION Initiative

An exciting commentary on Romans, very much designed to answer the questions of ordinary people. Those who want to use the material in a study group will find plenty of resources for engaging with the text.

David Peterson
Retired Principal of Oak Hill Theological College, London

WILLIAM TAYLOR
& DAVID DARGUE

# STYLE
## OR
# SUBSTANCE?

THE NATURE OF TRUE CHRISTIAN MINISTRY

ISBN 978-1-78191-229-4

# Style or Substance?

## *The Nature of True Christian Ministry*

### WILLIAM TAYLOR AND DAVID DARGUE

In every age, Christians experience pressure to embrace contemporary culture. In Corinth, the church had been infiltrated by some who had grown weary of the message of the cross: whose boast was in outward appearance. In 2 Corinthians 2-7, Paul writes into this setting, urging the Corinthians then, and us today, to embrace the 'weak' ministry of Gospel proclamation, to partner with 'weak' Christians, and to boast in 'weak' ministers. It is in this weakness that God's power is exhibited. Nothing could be more opposite to our celebrity culture.

These expositions ... are full of sane, sound, biblical instruction. I commend them highly, both as examples of faithful word ministry and as a necessary reminder that all lasting ministry will prioritize substance over style.

Kevin DeYoung
Senior Pastor, University Reformed Church, East Lansing, Michigan

In an age in which substance often gives way to style, we urgently need teaching like this, which builds convictions about the nature and power of authentic gospel ministry and spurs us to stick with it.

Vaughan Roberts
Rector of St Ebbe's, Oxford and Director of Proclamation Trust

David Dargue started out his training as an accountant, however has been serving Christ Church Newcastle since 2014. He is currently the minister at Christ Church, Gosforth.

# Christian Focus Publications

Our mission statement –

STAYING FAITHFUL

In dependence upon God we seek to impact the world through literature faithful to His infallible Word, the Bible. Our aim is to ensure that the Lord Jesus Christ is presented as the only hope to obtain forgiveness of sin, live a useful life and look forward to heaven with Him.

Our Books are published in four imprints:

## CHRISTIAN
## FOCUS

popular works including biographies, commentaries, basic doctrine and Christian living.

## CHRISTIAN
## HERITAGE

books representing some of the best material from the rich heritage of the church.

## MENTOR

books written at a level suitable for Bible College and seminary students, pastors, and other serious readers. The imprint includes commentaries, doctrinal studies, examination of current issues and church history.

## CF4•K

children's books for quality Bible teaching and for all age groups: Sunday school curriculum, puzzle and activity books; personal and family devotional titles, biographies and inspirational stories – Because you are never too young to know Jesus!

Christian Focus Publications Ltd,
Geanies House, Fearn, Ross-shire,
IV20 1TW, Scotland, United Kingdom.
www.christianfocus.com